HOW TO MAKE YOUR RELATIONSHIP WORK

HOW TO MAKE YOUR RELATIONSHIP WORK

Anne Geraghty

COLLINS & BROWN

Copyright © Vega 2003
Text copyright © Anne Geraghty 2003

First published in 2003 by Vega
This issue published in 2007 by
Collins & Brown
151 Freston Road
London
W10 6TH

An imprint of Anova Books Company Ltd

Distributed in the United States and Canada by
Sterling Publishing Co, 387 Park Avenue South, New York, NY 10016, USA

ISBN: 9 78184 340 408 8

A CIP catalogue record for this book is available from the British Library.

10 9 8 7 6 5 4 3 2 1

Printed and bound by Creative Print and Design, Ebbw Vale, Wales

This book can be ordered direct from the publisher.
Contact the marketing department, but try your bookshop first.

www.anovabooks.com

CONTENTS

Introduction

This book describes a new way of understanding intimate relationships. It focuses on how the love works in a relationship, rather than on the two individuals and what they do. It explains how love is a living force that affects not only ourselves and our partners, but exerts a powerful influence on the whole of our lives. It does not tell you what to do to make your relationships work, but how to let your love do it for you – and love does a far better job than we can. It shows you how to use your own love to create the relationship you long for.

This way of working with intimate sexual love came about because, after nine years, my partner and I found we could not be together and separated. Then we found we could not be apart and came back together. Despite both being therapists and undergoing years of intense self-exploration, including many forms of therapy, bodywork, group process, shamanistic rituals, meditations, and living in a Tantric Ashram and communities of various kinds, we were not able to resolve our differences. We were forced to find a greater power than our separate selves. This turned out to be our love.

During the next 12 years we learned how to tap into the power of our love and be guided by its wisdom, about ourselves and the relationship and for every area of our life. It has never failed us. Our life together has been transformed by the action of our own love working on and through us. Many of the individuals and couples who have worked with me in workshops and sessions have also found this way of working with relationships very helpful, deepening as it does their understanding and connection with their love. This book describes how you, too, can tap into the power of your own love to create the relationship and life you long for.

To understand that what happens in a relationship is love working to keep itself alive is a radical shift of perspective. As all new ways of understanding are difficult at first, parts of this book are challenging. Some chapters explain the nature of love; others are more practical with specific suggestions as to how to use your love to guide you. If you find the more general chapters do not interest you, turn to the more practical chapters first, then go back to the more explanatory chapters if you want to.

This book is more than a guide to living in loving relationships. The love that has helped my partner and me so much is also in this book. It helped to write it. And though you may not always agree with me, or have an experience that is different from what I describe, the deeper meaning of what love is trying to communicate will be understood by you. This is simply because you already know about love. We all do – we have yet to realise what we already know, that's all. I hope through this book that you will find as we have that the love that lives in your body, in your heart and in your soul can bring you all you long for. All we have to do is get out of our own way and let our love do the work.

THE NATURE OF LOVE

CHAPTER ONE

Love's Survival and Evolution

Love has taken away my practices
and piled me with poetry.
I used to be respectable and chaste and stable,
but who can stand in this strong wind
and remember those things?
JALAL AL-DIN RUMI (1207-1273)

What is love?

We can never describe or define love completely, as it is as complex and mysterious as life itself. Love is material, spiritual, animal and cosmic — a cultural and social phenomenon as well as an emotional and psychological one. It is the lifeblood of the invisible web of kinship that connects us and creates society, and the source of new life. It has inspired art, music and literature in every culture. Yet how much do we really know about the way love works?

For a start, love is a paradox. While being intimate and very private, it also has tremendous social consequences. It involves the anarchic instincts of our animal bodies and also our deepest spiritual longing. Like the other great paradoxical mysteries of our human condition — birth and death — sexual love is far greater than anything we think or say it is. Yet, even though we cannot explain it, we all know it, feel it and recognise it. We understand love by loving and being loved, by standing under it with our own experience. There is no other way. Our relationships are our teachers, and like all great teachings, some of the lessons will not be easy.

Intimate sexual relationships are deeply pleasurable but also painful. When we fall in love we long for so much, yet our hopes and dreams can be bitterly disappointed and we frequently end up hurt, resentful, distant, and even estranged from those we love, with no idea why. Love, something that matters so much to us, seems to be out of our control — a matter of luck or chance, rather than a profoundly human challenge in which we play the key part. The problem is not that we do not care enough, but that we do not understand how love works, and so when there are difficulties with our partners we become lost and confused as well as angry and hurt. Then it can seem that nothing we do makes any difference, however hard we try.

The key dynamic in intimate relationships is what is happening to the love.

Making an effort, compromise, a new way of communicating or some other process may ease conflict for a while, but before long the same problems often re-emerge in a different form that's even more difficult to resolve. We can solve fights about housework with a rota only to find the hidden power battle underlying the initial conflict shifts into fights about the children or finances. Talking things through, changing our behaviour, sharing how we feel, negotiating contracts, asserting ourselves and listening to each other are all helpful, but only up to a point. Strategies like these cannot always get to the root of the problem, which is – what is happening to the love?

Love is the currency of intimacy, the lifeblood, the energy, the *chi* of relationships. When love is flowing there is really no problem as the love will sort out the difficulties and naturally resolve the conflicts. Most fights during a honeymoon are easily forgotten and the making-up is pleasurable. But love often becomes stagnant or turns back on itself through accumulated hurts, various fears, social pressures, false beliefs, and other factors that undermine its natural workings. When this happens the love itself needs our attention.

What causes conflict is also what makes love

Dealing with difficulties by trying to do things differently or by simply changing our behaviour rarely works for very long anyway. When we impose our ideas of what should be happening onto a relationship, we interfere with the subtle and complex workings of love, and without meaning to can create more difficulties. We might believe that the responsibility for keeping the house tidy or keeping track of the finances must be shared equally. This will deal well with certain difficulties, such as if one simply expects the other to do it, or assumes that the other cannot, but it can also undermine the differences in skills and temperament that created the attraction in the first place. There needs to be a degree of sameness for there to be any meeting at all, but it is the difference that makes that meeting alive, interesting, sexual. And also what leads to the fights.

When we fall in love with someone who is not us, and therefore different, our love is continually challenged to go beyond itself, to extend beyond what we already know, into what is new, different and unknown. Loving what is the same is relatively easy; loving what is different is much harder. But it is much more satisfying, exciting, challenging, touching, turbulent, heart-opening, demanding, creative, wondrous, indescribable, terrifying, mysterious . . .

Love in a relationship is a set of interlinked, interdependent dynamics and balances, as complex as any ecosystem

Every intimate relationship has a complex ecology that needs to be respected.

If we simply try to do what we think is right, without first finding out what is happening to the love, then we run the risk of creating more trouble than we are trying to solve. There are several ways this can happen.

Firstly, we might interfere with how love is working in the relationship. What we think needs changing may actually be love trying to highlight something very important. A partner who shouts may be releasing the intolerable pressure from impossible demands, without really knowing why and so cannot articulate it. Without the shouting, their needs might be ignored, or they might leave, have a heart attack or hit out physically. Simply stopping the shouting will not help.

Secondly, we might rush to conclusions too soon and give the wrong medicine. Simply judging certain behaviours as wrong and trying to change them can make it much harder to find out *why* things are happening. For example, if you want your partner to listen to you, don't make a rule that they should; instead, listen to *them* and find out why they walk away. Besides, a rule that says you must always listen can mean you are forced to listen while the other attacks you, and that doesn't help much.

Thirdly, if either partner simply changes their behaviour without addressing the underlying cause, that cause does not just disappear, it merely goes underground and a deeper harm can result. If someone agrees to do something simply to keep the peace, they will usually take some form of revenge later, such as spending all weekend on the computer. Or if someone agrees never to shout, then they may end up depressed and withdrawn and not expressing themselves at all.

Our love can show us what the relationship needs

Some situations in relationships require immediate action – for example, when there is physical violence. Allopathic medicine, with its radical interventions (surgery, radiotherapy and intensive drug treatment) is brilliant in a crisis, where it's a matter of life and death. But other healing traditions, such as herbalism, Ayurveda, Chinese medicine and Naturopathy, are better at prevention, maintaining good health, and at healing the roots of disorders. These older traditions listen to the *whole* body to learn what is the underlying nature of the disease. They do not treat only the symptoms.

In the same way, for the health of our relationships, we need love itself to reveal to us what is needed from the whole picture, rather than imposing our ideas on the relationship prematurely. Love can show us how to make changes that do not interfere with the subtle and complex balances of intimate relationship. For example, when things are difficult in intimate relationships, sometimes not doing something is more useful than doing something. It may be more important to let things be than to change things. Sitting in uncertainty, without immediately doing something, allows aspects of the situation to be revealed that could be missed otherwise.

> *A woman was offered a prestigious, well-paid job that would involve uprooting the whole family to another city. When she and her partner began a discussion about the job, with each stating what they wanted and defining their personal goals, they found themselves arguing. This negotiating style, useful in some situations, did not suit the complex intimacy of their relationship. But when they began by each acknowledging that they did not know what was the best or right thing to do, a much deeper discussion ensued. Sitting together in uncertainty, allowing themselves to be confused and not to know, and without reaching any immediate solution or action, their hopes and fears for themselves, each other, the children and their whole situation were able to emerge. A decision evolved slowly that took into account everything that mattered to them, their future goals included.*

It makes sense in many situations to use power and control to get what we need, but in intimate relationships it may be more important to be vulnerable than powerful, more appropriate to allow ourselves not to know than to be right. Taking care of our love can involve giving way to the needs of a greater reality than our immediate personal wishes. In this example the needs of the family were more important than the immediate wish of either parent.

In later chapters we will look at how to learn from and be guided by love, when to assert your own needs and when to give way to the needs of the relationship.

Love, like life, continuously works to remain alive

The love that can teach us *how* to love is clearly far more than mutual liking, simple sexual attraction and warm feelings towards each other. It is a powerful and turbulent force that is both at the root of our human predicament and its creative resolution. To make love is to be involved in the very creative act that made us and which is the fact of our life. Sexual love is therefore at the heart of our human mystery, both personally and collectively, and however much we want to know what love is, ultimately it will defy all analysis and explanation. So, while knowing that we will never understand love completely, and would not want to, let us explore some of the attributes of this profoundly human yet essentially mysterious energy.

All life remains alive through continually balancing metabolic processes to keep our organs, hormones, muscles and nervous system all working within the parameters that sustain life. If our body temperature rises too high, our blood sugar drops too low, our glands go into overdrive, or any one of a multitude of bodily functions goes outside the balance that maintains life, then we are in danger of dying. The body maintains this balance through a complex homeostasis that is continually at work to keep us healthy.

Even when there has been major trauma or damage, this process continues. Other organs will take on a degree of the function of whatever organ is failing, other glands will produce some of the missing hormone, and other parts of the brain will take on the functions of what has been damaged. The body will always attempt to maintain itself in equilibrium. Life struggles continuously to remain alive in a dynamic homeostasis. Even the Earth itself has been described as a biosphere working like a living organism to maintain itself in balance. Love works within our relationships in the same way. Like life, love continuously works to remain alive and in balance.

Love is a living energy and, although invisible, is as real as what we can see and touch. And in its struggles to remain alive and growing, love, like all life, evolves in complexity, richness and diversity. The conflict and confusion we experience with our partners is love working to survive and grow – though it rarely feels like this when in the middle of a fight.

We tend to conclude when there is conflict and pain, that something is wrong, that it should not be like this, and then we either try to fix it or walk away. But at a deeper level there is nothing wrong. It is exactly at the points of conflict, rage and misunderstanding that there is the potential to extend beyond our current limitations, to expand our understanding, to go beyond whatever is restricting our capacity for love. We can, in fact, use conflict to make more love.

Everything happening in a relationship is a manifestation of love struggling to maintain the dynamic homeostasis of life; love trying to come into form through us. Attempting to fix things before we have found out what love is trying to teach us can therefore interfere with what needs to happen. If we first understand the underlying patterns and designs of love, we can respond to what is really needed rather than trying to force ourselves or our partners to change in ways we think we should, and which may make things more difficult in the long term.

Sometimes our understanding and awareness alone is enough to bring love back into balance. Sometimes we are forced into heartbreak and despair before love can come through. But even when we interfere with love, there is no blame or condemnation from our love. Our love unconditionally loves us. Which makes learning from the relationship much easier than learning from our partners, who naturally have their hidden agendas and vested interests, just as we do.

Love needs us as much as we need love

The love we make with our partners can teach us many things, yet, powerful as it is, love needs us for its creation, sustenance and fulfillment as much as we need love for *our* creation, sustenance and fulfillment. Rather than taking love for granted, assuming it simply does its thing without needing anything from us, when we understand how love works we can begin to work *with* love rather than against it. Understanding the nature of love and how it constantly strives to remain alive through hidden patterns, harmonies, symmetries, synchronicities and reciprocities, not only gives us useful knowledge, it makes living in intimate sexual relationships happier, richer, easier. All we have to do is get out of our own way and let love do the work. But, like with other deceptively simple suggestions to 'be yourself, 'just relax', 'be happy, don't worry', there are many things that need to happen first.

One key thing love needs from us is our understanding. In the first section of this book we explore the nature of love generally. You might wonder why the bigger picture, the social, cultural and biological aspects of love are as important for our sexual relationships as more personal and psychological ones, but no relationship is an island. Even in our most intimate moments, what we experience is affected by our culture, our language, our biology, our conditioning and the society we live in. To understand how loving relationships work, we cannot ignore these other dimensions. Besides which, knowing that love has levels and complexities beyond just the two of you helps greatly in times of trouble:

1 The pressure comes off, as we are less likely to rush in with simple solutions that can make matters worse.

2 We stop comparing ourselves to media images and Hollywood versions of intimate sexual love – amazing sex every time, subtle lighting, arguments in dazzling sound bites – because we know that a perfect love life is impossible. Plus, we know why.

3 We feel less of a failure when there are difficulties, as we know it is not totally our fault. This makes us more willing to deal with what is going on rather than

avoiding it out of shame or guilt.

4   Knowing that conflict and difficulties have aspects that are nothing to do with us personally means we are less likely to judge and blame our partners.

5   Instead of trying to stop the conflict at all costs, we can allow what is happening to reveal its deeper levels.

6   We understand what is happening before prematurely trying to fix it.

7   Understanding a situation reduces anxiety. The chaos, confusion and turbulence begins to have meaning, and we no longer feel we must be crazy or foolish to be living in such a chaotic, confusing and turbulent manner, simply because, in our different ways, we all are.

8   By understanding how intimacy and society affect one another – the local and global being intimately related – we realise that human sexual love is profoundly intimate and yet with more universal significance than we might ever have imagined. As a result we begin to give our love the respect it deserves.

Now let's travel the world and the seven seas and see how everybody's grappling with something when it comes to love.

CHAPTER TWO

Seven Seas, Seven Heavens

There is no companion but love
No starting, or finishing, yet, a road.
RUMI

There are seven aspects of human sexual love, each of which presents us with a challenge. The sea is always salty, wherever we taste it, and these seven aspects – uniqueness, complexity, vulnerability, interdependence, surrender, sexuality and transcendence – have relevance for us all, whatever may be the qualities of our particular relationship. The challenge is to make enough love to journey through the struggle and turmoil of our human condition to whatever heaven is waiting for us on the other side. We may meet sharks and get shipwrecked while swimming around in these deep waters, but we may also find coral reefs and paradise.

1 Uniqueness: each relationship is unique

Although human love has universal aspects, there are significant ways in which each relationship is like no other. Each relationship is unique and each love also. There is no other love on the planet like yours. There never has been and never will be again, which makes your love both precious and alone.

Through the uniqueness of each snowflake, each fingerprint, each genetic code, through each moment in time and each relationship, life continually renews itself, always evolving into new forms. This uniqueness is essential for sexual love, as without it the rules for how to behave in love would have been discovered long ago and written in stone. Love would become like driving or doing the laundry, only superficial details would change. Our love would be merely a copy of other loves, all relationships echoes of each other, with no specialness to our love, no surprises, no adventure, no risk, no excitement. The infinite variety of relationships is absolutely essential to love.

No-one therefore, other than the couple themselves, *really* knows what is going on in the heart of an intimate relationship. Others may be able to offer insights or useful suggestions, but ultimately the only experts on the relationship are the couple themselves and their love. Love is not like carpentry where a craftsman can tell us exactly how to dovetail a joint or hammer in a nail (though it's likely that a master carpenter would say each piece of wood is unique and that there is no one right way to hammer in a nail).

But if no-one truly knows a relationship other than the two involved, and there is no expert with the answers, who or what can we turn to when we need help? It has to be something intimately connected with both partners, yet greater than either individually. Our love is exactly this.

Most of what we say is in the form of unique sentences that have never been said or heard before, yet despite this we understand them. This is because a deeper grammar allows us to both generate sentences and decipher them. Some have called this a language instinct, some the universal grammar of meaning, but whatever you call it there has to be a deeper pattern to language than the surface structures, otherwise we would not be able to understand a sentence we have never heard before. In the same way, there is a deeper grammar generating what we observe in relationships, and even though each relationship is unique, there are general patterns to be found in the deeper structure. This deeper grammar is love. The patterns are the symmetries, synchronicities, balances, equivalencies in the way loving relationships work that can only be seen when we look at the relationship as a whole, and not just at the two individuals. Though the ways in which these general patterns reveal themselves is again unique for each relationship.

Knowing these patterns makes all the difference. We can then use this knowledge to tap into the wisdom of love as a guide in our own unique relationship. And when we take on board the unique and singular qualities of our love, we will value and care for it all the more.

2. Complexity: every relationship has a complex and diverse ecology

There are many ways of loving, and love has many aspects even within the one relationship. What nurtures one aspect of our love does not therefore necessarily help another. This diversity and complexity needs to be respected before trying to change things, otherwise, with the best of intentions, we can end up interfering with the natural ways in which love works, and creating more trouble than we were trying to solve.

When the birds in China were found to be eating a portion of the crops every year, they were all killed. That year there was a record harvest. The next year, however, the crops were completely destroyed by the insects that had previously been eaten by the birds. There were no crops and no birdsong. Because of the scarcity of food, people were ordered to kill their pet dogs. The losses mounted.

Just as with nature, before recommending what should happen in a relationship, we need to respect the complex and diverse ecology of love. Rules for how to make relationships work can, for example, bury important processes that need to come to light. Yet we need rules that govern behaviour, otherwise we would not be able to live together and there would be chaos not community. These rules must be flexible and open to negotiation as circumstances change, especially in intimate relationships where changes occur often, maybe daily, even moment to moment.

Rules between lovers are most useful when they create a safe arena to be free and spontaneous, not when they are ends in themselves. At the heart of sexual passion is spontaneity and freedom, not conformity to rules and discipline. Rules that control the expression of feeling may be a part of this, but rules that control who we are and what we feel will never work. An agreement to be polite to each other's friends might make sense, but a rule to like each other's friends does not. Just as rules about sexual activity with others protect the relationship, ones that prohibit any sexual feeling to others will undermine it.

However sincere we are, controlling the natural flow of love by attempting to eliminate thoughts and feelings that we think are damaging to our love will not work in the long term. A more radical and organic process is needed to deal with difficulties in intimate sexual relationships, such as using our own love to show us what is needed. Tapping into the wisdom and knowledge of your own love may be the single most important tool you find to make your intimate relationships happy and fulfilling.

3. Vulnerability: the power needed in the world is opposite to the vulnerability needed in intimacy

The skills we learned as children to develop our power and self-protection were necessary for us to grow into adults and make our own way in the world. Without developing power and control over first ourselves and then others, we would be at the mercy of whatever happened and be unable to survive. We would not be able to create anything or support ourselves and those who depend on us. Intimacy, however, involves very different processes – being with another without doing anything, letting go of control, having no protective barrier to separate us, and dissolving the boundaries between self and other. But when we let down our defences, we become vulnerable, literally able to be wounded. This makes intimacy both something we long for and something we are afraid of.

Loving someone makes us vulnerable to another person who we cannot ultimately control. They will always insist upon being themselves and not what we want them to be. They will do it their way. They will have a life of their own as well as a life with us. Many of the fights we have with our partners come from our attempts to control them, and their natural resistance. And vice versa. And they will continue to do so until eventually we understand that freedom, both for ourselves and our partners, is an essential part of love. But it takes a lot of love and a lot of fights to realise this.

From the deep vulnerability and surrender with which we began life as a baby, we struggle to become a separate autonomous individual with power and control over life, only to return to vulnerability and surrender in the intimacy of sexual love. Our first vulnerability to love is out of biological necessity; our later surrender comes only after many struggles. Like all great journeys, we end where we began, the difference being not in the place, but in us. By the time we surrender to love again, we have been transformed by our own love. Love always brings us to more love.

4. Interdependence: no-one, and no relationship, is an island

However hard we try, we cannot escape the fact that we need others, just as others need us. Our culture however emphasises the rights and freedom of the individual far more than the responsibilities and interdependencies of community and family. Historically, this respect for the individual has been very important. It has taught us to value the intrinsic worth of every one of us. It has given each of us the dignity and rights of freedom. Yet there also needs to be integration between the rights of the individual and the responsibilities of community, which is an ongoing challenge for humanity as a whole as well as for individuals.

In sexual relationships we are confronted by the challenge to integrate the needs of the self with those of others – how to be both separate and together, how to respect both the 'I' and the 'we' – more intimately than anywhere else. And if we cannot work it out at home, how can we hope to work it out on the bigger stage globally? Yet most of us find it hard to think beyond what we ourselves need and be sensitive to what the relationship needs.

One reason why this is difficult is that we think of ourselves primarily as separate individuals. Just as important, however, are the *relationships* that create society. It may be that the invisible worldwide web of relationships is even more elemental than the separate selves. Physicists now say matter itself is created out of a network of relationships and not, as previously thought, out of individual sub-atomic particles or charges of energy. A completely new explanation had to be found in quantum physics for why events happened before their causes came into being, and why particles could be in two places at once, or could disappear and reappear in different places at random. Normal conceptions of space, time and causality were abandoned, and the only explanation for what was observed was that the most significant entities were not the individual particles or charges of energy themselves, but the *relationships* between them. Relationships not only matter – now, it seems, they *are* matter.

As soon as we appreciate that relationships are forces and elements in their own right, the subtle patterns, synchronicities and balances found in intimate relationships can more easily be seen as the workings of an overarching intelligence – love. However, we are also faced with yet another challenge, how to meet not only our own needs and those of our partners, but also the needs of the relationship. What teaches us when to give way to the needs of the relationship and when to assert our own separate needs, when to step aside and when to stand our ground, are the struggles and fights we have with our partners. There is no other way. Our differences with our partners are exactly what will cause trouble and exactly what will force our love to grow beyond itself.

Each one of us struggles in an intimate relationship with the raw necessity to expand our sense of self until our 'I' becomes a 'we'. Then what matters to one is what matters to both. The expansion of 'I' into 'we' is crucial in intimate relationships, and is also a struggle we are confronted with collectively. Dividing the human family into 'us' and 'them' does not really serve anyone. It ignores our common humanity and the greater 'we' that includes all of us. Creating dialogue and building bridges is important for nations, religions and communities as well as families and couples. The love that is greater than our separate egos, that embraces both self and other, that contains all polarities, is in short supply globally and locally, yet is very much needed. And this love, possibly the greatest untapped energy resource of our planet, begins at home.

5. Surrender: love asks even more of us than we ask of love

We tend to expect love to give us what we need and forget to think about what love needs from us. Love will nurture us when we nurture love. There is a reciprocity here. But we have absorbed a romantic fallacy that intimate sexual relationships will automatically bring us happiness, fulfillment, comfort, security and fun. When they do not, we conclude that we are with the wrong partner or are doing something wrong. But when difficulties arise in relationships, this is always love at work in some way. Everything happening in intimate relationships, including the fights, is love trying to remain alive and free, trying to bring the relationship back into balance by revealing what is needed. Trying to make our relationship how we think it should be, and trying to find out what our love is trying to achieve, are radically different approaches. The first is about developing power and control over love; the second involves a commitment and surrender to love.

We cannot control love anyway. Love is a far greater force in life than that of our conscious ego or individual mind, which is partly why it is so difficult to explain how love works, yet not at all difficult to experience it. One way of looking at love is to think of it as a field of energy, underlying the material world we perceive with our five senses.

The hidden source of physical reality, the realm of energy, has been given many names – the Tao, the Dhamma, the quantum energy field, the spirit world, and Dreamtime. But whatever name we call it, from this energetic realm love causes certain things to happen in our intimate relationships in the same way physicists are now suggesting reality itself is a field of energy that manifests itself through constantly changing forms.

Love seems to work in ways similar to what biologists have described as 'morphic resonance'. Traditional reductionist science cannot explain many of the phenomena of nature, such as how an embryo grows, how termites build nests, how a flock of birds behave as one organism, how life itself evolved into such rich and complex diversity. Some biologists have concluded that there is an overarching intelligence at work that cannot be explained by analysing and reducing processes to their component parts. They have suggested there is a force field that works like an invisible blueprint, shaping life rather like a magnetic field creates shapes in iron filings. Love seems to work in a similar way within intimate relationships, creating the patterns of synchronicity, symmetry, reciprocity and dynamic homeostasis that run through the life of a relationship. The overarching intelligence here is love.

The energy of love is so powerful that ultimately love asks even more of us than we ask of love. Love demands our complete surrender. It is to the higher power of love that we will surrender anyway – at death, if not before. Love is our legacy to those close to us, and our final gift back to life, and though our bodies may die our love lives on in life forever. Love has a power and a glory far greater than we realise. Deep sexual love reveals this, but only when we surrender to it.

6. Sexuality: the animal instincts of the body are outlawed by society yet integral to sexual love

Sexual love is intense because sexual love involves the animal instincts of our bodies, and the animal is totally committed to life. With no self-consciousness and thought to interfere with its immediate and total spontaneity, the integrity of the animal lies in every moment it is alive. Such innocent bodily totality is naturally intense.

Our animal body is the seat of the unconscious. Every impulse, desire, instinct and feeling that we humans have learned to control and repress in order that we behave in ways that are acceptable to others do not just disappear. They are held and controlled through tensions in the muscular system. In sexual love, in the intimacy between two bodies, the unconscious energies of both are also meeting. Whatever may be happening above the table, there are unknown worlds meeting beneath it. When two people make love, therefore, there are far more things coming together than we know – two worlds, not only two persons.

This coming together of so many energies and aspects can disorient and disturb us, change everything and threaten our freedom. It can also make us more alive, create new life and, of course, make love. We naturally want the delights of intimacy but, equally naturally, not the turbulence and disturbance. Yet we cannot have one without the other.

Making love brings feeling and sensation back into the body. Its very physicality awakens the passions and intense feelings we have learned to keep firmly in check since our early childhood. Often the energies involved in sexual love are the very ones we are afraid will most harm our love – selfishness, aggression, desire, strong feelings of possessiveness, jealousy and need. And with these often come anger and fear. Yet these return anyway once awoken by sexual love and, however much we try to be loving and caring, we will at times hate most the one we love most.

This intensity of feeling can make us afraid. Cutting off does not work as this shuts down our energy and with it our sexuality, while expressing our feelings with no restraint leads to chaos and violence. So the problem becomes how to allow and express such feelings without overwhelming either ourselves or our partners. Once again our love can help by providing the context within which threatening feelings can be contained (and therefore safe), yet also expressed (and therefore released). We will be looking at this later.

The surrender into the instincts of the body in sexual love requires us to go beyond our minds and personalities and into the instincts and energies of the unconscious, where different realities and energies from those known to our intellectual minds are experienced. The intellectual mind organises life into separate distinct entities, dividing life in order to rule over it. The body knows no such alienating separation, and neither does love.

Love is an energy that permeates existence, but only sexual love makes that love material. Sexual love brings love into the body, makes it flesh, and in the holy communion of sexual love the most earthy and animal becomes the most sacred and spiritual – incarnation not transcendence is what it's all about. Making love, literally, makes us love.

7. Transcendence: love is beyond our personalities and our minds

Our brilliant human minds have evolved in ways that enable us to create maps of reality, consisting of things and the ways in which they affect each other through chains of cause and effect. This has led to the development of a science and a technology that allows most of us in the post-industrialised West to live in comfort, no longer having to struggle for survival. This way of thinking, however, has made it harder for us to understand the workings of love. Love involves a flow of energy rather than discreet objects, an energetic reality rather than a material one. But it is hard to change the way we think about things and the more concrete ways we have been taught to see reality. This is despite the fact that falling in love in the first place is connected with our energy, instincts and feelings, not our intellect, mind or thoughts. To attune to the formless worlds of energy and feeling we therefore need to think in new and different ways about love.

When people love each other, their loving creates an energy field around them. This is love. Love is not an abstract concept but a real living force. Over time a couple creates a body of love that becomes not only a source of support, wisdom, pleasure and healing, but through the power of the energy field actually creates situations and events in their lives. For example, love will bring to the surface anything that is interfering or blocking the flow of energy. It will create the ongoing balance a relationship needs in order to survive. It will bring into form manifestations of our love so that we can know and become available to yet more love. Clearly we are talking here about a greater force than the sweet togetherness of mutual support, though hopefully that is present, too. This love is ruthless in the pursuit of truth, freedom and yet more love. Love, as well as taking us on a honeymoon, will force us to encounter our worst nightmares, deepest fears, and if necessary will break our hearts in order that we open to the ultimate truth of love.

This love is a potent force that will challenge us, force us to be real, take us through the frontiers of our fear and into the unknown. It is a higher power than our ego and brings us to life so completely (and this means the worst as well as the best of us) that we are transformed. This love reveals profound truths about ourselves, our partners and the soul of humanity. It brings each of us to our own unique fulfillment and destiny, as love is intrinsic to who and what we are. Such a love does not come easy. Like all births there is a labour to be gone through before it can arrive in form, in the body of our intimate relationships.

Intimate sexual love gives birth to a body of love so powerful that it can eventually contain not only the couple, their children and those around them, but can embrace the whole of life. The Tantric enlightenment is exactly this – to make enough love to contain existence itself, to give birth to love in the body, to become love. And though we may not be called to give up everything and live in a cemetery dancing on graves, as did the first Tantric couple, Saraha and Tamulkha, we are all called upon to love in some form or other.

CHAPTER THREE

Kinds of Loving

Whoever finds love
beneath hurt and grief
disappears into emptiness
with a thousand new disguises.
RUMI

Each relationship is unique, unlike any other, and every relationship has archetypal aspects that are the same for us all. This makes human love profoundly universal and impersonal, as well as intensely intimate and personal. And in what is closest to us and most familiar, we also find what is remote and extraordinary. As a consequence, life with our sexual partners is rich, fulfilling, complex and creative but also confusing, turbulent and difficult. This is especially these days, when we tend to look for nourishment, support, pleasure, understanding, emotional closeness, passion, a lover, co-parent, dancing partner, best friend, fellow traveller and more all within the one partnership. There are many ways to love and be loved.

It helps to have some kind of map describing different kinds of love, even though this can never accommodate the rich bio-diversity of real relationships. Intimate sexual love appears to have five basic forms, each one holding a different understanding of relationships: instinctual love, romantic love, reciprocal love, redemptive love and transcendental love. We make many different kinds of love within one relationship, and most relationships have a combination of these forms of love in their make-up. Usually, however, there will be one or two more dominant.

It is very easy to make assumptions that how we experience love is the only way. For example, we may think that intimate sexual love is about being close and taking care of one another, when for another couple it is about being partners and working side by side to create a life together. One couple might see love as primarily being about security and comfort in a harsh world, while another sees love as an on-going in-depth exploration of themselves and life. Knowing more about the different forms of love can ease anxiety and pressures within our own relationships as we begin to accept these differences are natural and inevitable. We stop comparing our own relationships with those of others and feel free to create a relationship that suits us rather than conforming to some ideal.

Instinctual Love

Instinctual love has little awareness of the inner workings of the relationship, and love is not seen as something to be explored or reflected upon. Young children love in this way, as do some animals. The young of all mammals instinctively bond with their parents, and their instinctive 'love' is reciprocated in the parents' bonding with their offspring, that is unless something disturbs this process. There is a natural bonding of some kind with all who belong in a family, that is, those bodies that are familiar to each other. This bonding is an intense attachment. Very young children, for example, will go to their death rather than leave their parents. In adult sexual relationships this instinctive bonding is an important aspect of love, primarily because the drives and passions of the instinctual forces are at the very heart of sexual intimacy. Hence, the possessive rage, intense longing, jealous passion, irrational fears and fierce loyalties that can arise between lovers far more than in other relationships.

Instinctive love is a profoundly selfish love, but innocently so. Partners with a great deal of instinctual love are spontaneously real with each other and have an integrity and transparent honesty, but little conscious empathy or sensitivity to the other. If they remain together, a fierce loyalty develops, but when there is conflict, this is more acted out than reflected upon. This can lead to sexual addictions or uncomprehending violence in its destructive form. But then, all forms of human love on this bi-polar planet seem to have both creative and destructive aspects, and in its most creative form instinctual love is charismatic, passionate and energetically very alive.

Wherever people are together a bonding of some kind will always develop over time, a form of instinctual love whether we are aware of it or not. It is simply in the nature of the body to bond with those around us, and is therefore to some extent present in all relationships that involve the body. There is a degree of this instinctual bonding even between different species that share the same habitat. Some animals will save the lives of individuals from other species with which they are familiar. Hippos have been seen to rescue small animals from crocodiles. Dolphins have saved humans from drowning. A lioness in Africa has adopted two young antelope and fed them rather than eating them. You could say instinctual love is the invisible web that maintains all life on this planet. It is certainly the force at the root of sexual love.

We all have many parts, and in sexual partnerships these many aspects are involved with the many aspects of our partners. There are therefore many relationships, many dynamics, within the one relationship. The parts of us involved in instinctual love are our child parts, our animal instincts, our non-rational feelings and our sexual energies. Couples with a great deal of instinctual love in the make-up of their relationships will experiment with sex, have intense sexual feelings, play sexually with each other, and maybe stay in bed all day. They will also tend to find explanations, analyses, insight and talking about things not really very helpful. What is usually far more important is a safe place to allow their energy to run free. Asking more instinctive people to reflect on why they are behaving in a certain way just makes things more tangled, and is not needed anyway once the love is flowing. And, of course, in the subtle bio-diversity of love, intellectual and self-reflective types and instinctive-feeling types are often attracted to each other – yet another scenario for misunderstanding and conflict as well as learning and expansion.

When there is relatively little instinctual love in a relationship the sexual passion will be weak and not so important for the couple. Other intimacies may matter more, such as emotional closeness, a dialogue of ideas or a political comradeship. When a high proportion of instinctive love is present there is the potential for it to evolve into a love of great wisdom and generosity. Love will always transform itself into its own highest fulfillment. This involves love expanding until it can incorporate its polar opposite, so what was once outside the love can then be contained within it (but more about this later). Here, the most self-centred love can become the most self-transcendent.

Romantic Love

Romantic love, unlike instinctual love, has an *idea* of love, though this tends to be idealised, where the beloved is seen as perfect. Such perfection requires a perfect love and this is the romantic ideal of total devotion to the other, such as the courtly love of a knight, the surrender of a disciple for the guru, and the fan's adoration of the star. This (allegedly) selfless love has no object other than serving the other, and delights in the pleasure and happiness it can give. It is the opposite pole to instinctual love.

When romantic love is a major part of an intimate sexual relationship there are unexpected gifts, surprises, poetry, exotic holidays, candle-lit dinners, or whatever else are the ways a couple has of celebrating the specialness of each other. The individuals have a sense of how unique their love is, how they feel made for each other, and how their love seems the fulfillment of a destiny and is no ordinary thing. When there is conflict and trouble, or the normal irritations of daily routine, however, they tend to assume that something must be wrong, and that there would be no difficulties otherwise. They may think: 'I am with the wrong person', 'I have done something wrong', or 'The magic has gone'. When the romantic view of love dominates a relationship, it is assumed there is very little that can be done about conflict – you either endure it or walk away.

Many traditional marriages fall into this mode. Time together wears away the unreal romantic picture, and if there is enough love between them, the couple create a love that is caring and companionable, and which they both value and are nourished by. A love that is alive will always expand to enfold more and more in its embrace, including, particularly, whatever we may have once rejected. As before, the love made in such a relationship is often the opposite of its romantic beginning, being extremely pragmatic, forgiving faults and accepting imperfection. If, however, there is not enough love between them, then the couple can end up resigned and disappointed or resentful and bitter.

In relationship counselling, couples for whom this dimension of love is very important, like to be given specific suggestions as to what to do to reconnect them with the magic which is, of course, their love. They may then go on a dinner date as if they were meeting for the first time, give the other a gift that represents their love, write a letter describing a time when they felt close to the other, or say positive things to each other. They may even try rephrasing habitual complaints. So, instead of, for instance, 'You're always late home, I clearly don't matter to you as much as your work', they may say, 'I've been looking forward to seeing you and found it hard to wait'. Similar suggestions to other couples may not be welcome and be seen as interfering or controlling.

Romantic love can inspire us to great acts of self-transcendence and sacrifice. It can fuel a devotion to our partners' welfare that can help carry us through the turbulent times when we need all the help we can get. And, especially at the beginning of a relationship, the romantic dream is a potent force for bringing us together with our partners in the first place. All human sexual love has a component of romance in its make-up. Thank goodness. Without enough romantic love the music fades and there is no more dancing.

Reciprocal Love

A more pragmatic love, reciprocal love, recognises the human frailties in us all and does not seek perfection. And, anyway, the man that went looking all over the world for the perfect partner, refusing all the imperfect love that came his way, eventually, as an old man, found her, only to have her turn away from his obvious imperfection.

Reciprocal love sees relationships as a transactional exchange where there's the possibility of both partners getting what they need and want from each other if they work at it. Conflict is seen as a symptom of trouble that needs sorting out using various processes to help the communication. The two make contracts, agreements and negotiate to maximise what each gets from the relationship. Compromises are made and fair exchanges worked out so that there's a balance of give and take. Most Couples

Counselling and 'How to Do It' relationship manuals use this transactional model of relationship dynamics. The counsellor or therapist creates a safe and supportive atmosphere where each person in turn is encouraged to share how they feel, listen to each other and work out how to meet each other's needs. This model encourages communication, contractual agreements and a willingness to compromise.

When conflict and trouble are not resolved using these methods, it is assumed that one or the other or both is doing something wrong. Perhaps they are not revealing enough, not committed enough, not taking enough risks, not letting go enough, or in some other way are not doing enough to make it work. Unlike romantic and instinctual love, where it is assumed we have very little or no control over the forces and feelings of love, here the opposite is assumed, that we have the power to control love. Just as we have assumed our modern technology can control nature, in this kind of loving we expect to be able to control love. All we have to do is work out what to do and how to do it, and the relationship will work. And, just as technology has brought great benefits, this approach can lead to deeper communication and mutual understanding. But it can also lead to a nightmare, as sometimes can our technological interference with nature.

For example, the relationship can become a relentless pursuit of what to do to bring back the love, and we can work on ourselves in a remorseless and seemingly endless struggle to find out what is wrong and put it right. Like nature, however, there is an aspect of love that requires us to surrender ourselves. Love is ultimately a higher power than our separate individual egos, and though we may fight it, love will continue to confront us with the limitations of our power to control things, especially with our sexual partners. When reciprocal love is dominant, this can lead to a lack of respect for the powerful anarchic forces of sexuality. We may try to make our sexuality conform to our various agreements and ideologies, but human sexuality will never conform completely to rules and contracts, without diminishing itself. The sexual expression of love will weaken or become distorted if we try to dominate and control it without respect, however well-meaning we are.

Reciprocal love respects both the self and the other, and tries to maximise the happiness of each. It has a practical and pragmatic approach to love that can be very useful, especially when there is a home to be run, children to be cared for, careers to be built, and bills to be paid. Again, there will be a component of this form of love in every committed sexual relationship where two people are creating a life together. Without enough of this love, a couple will find life lacks stability and coherence. Plans will not reach fruition and they will have trouble building a future together. Perhaps not surprisingly, reciprocal love plays a large part in most modern relationships, with our emphasis on mutual understanding, material security and comfortable family life. Reciprocal love as it grows seems to evolve into an appreciation of relaxing and simply *being* together. Perhaps after so many years of doing things – working on the relationship, making arrangements, contracts, agreements, etc – the simple lightness of being together is especially pleasurable. Again, love, in its great wisdom, brings into being the opposite polarity from where it began.

Redemptive Love

When two partners are attuned to the psychological world, then another kind of loving evolves, a love that explores these inner realities, a redemptive love. Here it is understood that each person brings to the relationship a set of complex inner dynamics that influence the relationship, often without either partner being aware of what is going on. Within the relationship there is an on-going exploration of what is happening as part of a journey both are making into their inner worlds. Conflict is seen as an indication that each needs to explore themselves and discover the ways they defend themselves from their partner, the baggage they bring from other relationships, and their unconscious desires to destroy the relationship. A relationship is seen as a journey that involves a voyage of self-discovery through an exploration of the past, especially our childhoods, our parents' relationship, previous sexual experiences, and our hopes and fears about love. The idea behind this is that once we have become aware of unconscious patterns of relating, they can no longer operate destructively with our partners.

Here, the partners will not necessarily wait until there's trouble before exploring themselves. They will often engage in psychotherapy, group therapy or some other form of healing on an on-going basis. Once released from being trapped in unresolved issues, we are free to love our partners in the here and now, and are more aware of some of the unconscious dynamics that were undermining our capacity for love. This model assumes that if trouble and conflict continue, then one or other or both partners are not yet clear of the past, that there is some unconscious fear or anger or unresolved conflict blocking the love. The process then involves an inner exploration to bring the unconscious dynamic to light, where it can be dealt with.

Redemptive love is a potent process. It brings to light many aspects of each person's psyche, and leads to deep insight and self-knowledge. It is a love that, in the search of the self, makes partners comrades as well as lovers. A sexual relationship that has this dimension to its process is a deep and powerful one, though if there is an imbalance, relentless self-revelation can lead to the two becoming therapists for each other rather than lovers. One of the great rewards of this kind of love is the evolution of a wordless understanding between the two. After so many years committed to becoming aware of and giving voice to their inner process, bringing to light their unconscious patterns, they grow to enjoy a profound silence and stillness, sitting together in the dark simplicity of being. Again, love has expanded to include its opposite pole, and in doing so builds yet another bridge across the great divide.

Transcendental Love

Up until this point we have had a sense of love being between two separate individuals who come together, form a relationship and engage in various types of dialogue and communication with many personal dynamics within and between them. There is also an assumption running through all these different aspects of love that when there is conflict, trouble and pain, something is wrong. There is another aspect of love, however, that sees thing very differently.

Transcendental love contains all the loves previously described and is greater than them all. Transcendental love is the energy field of love that is created when people love each other, whatever the kind of loving. From this viewpoint, the focus is on the love rather than the two individuals, because what happens in intimate relationships is determined by the love just as much as by the two individuals.

A body of love evolves over time between lovers that is as real as any other body and conforms to some of the same laws, though it consists of energy not matter. Each kind of loving creates a different quality to the energy field of this love-body, which in turn affects the way the relationship evolves. This is hard for us to understand as we tend to think of reality as being composed of concrete objects in time and space. And so the energy body of love does not therefore seem like a real living body to us. But reality is more than the material. There is a whole domain of existence that is energy not matter, and this is where the energy field or body of love works from. I will return to all of this, in much greater depth, later.

From this perspective, love is understood to be alive and doing all it can to remain alive, as do living creatures everywhere. Conflict is not seen as something *wrong*, but a manifestation of love seeking to maintain a dynamic balance between all the energies and forces of the relationship, so that they do not blow it apart. Just as life has a homeostatic drive to reduce the tension of imbalance – when we are hungry we seek food, when tired we sleep, when cold we seek warmth, and so on. This maintains a dynamic balance between all the energies and forces that together make up life, yet also continuously threaten death. Conflict and distress, therefore, is a manifestation of love's attempt to remain alive, in balance and growing. When a tree grows leaning to the east, it is not a sign that the tree is doing something wrong – it is simply a natural response to the prevailing westerly wind, and in this way the tree protects itself from the harmful effects of gales. And when, every spring, seeds sprout and plants push up through the soil, nature is maintaining a balance between all living things and their habitats. If, for some reason, a plant does not grow, it is not that the plant is doing something wrong, but that the right conditions for its growth are not in place.

When it comes to the ecology of our intimate relationships, however, it is easy to assume when there is trouble that this is a sign of something wrong and that it shouldn't be like this. The tree should not be leaning east, it should be straight. Looking at relationships from another dimension, however, there is never anything wrong, just a dynamic to be explored. The exploration is out of the realm of right and wrong, which means that the couple can start to become interested in finding out what is going on rather than trying desperately to get it right. It also means there is no-one to blame, which reduces self-righteousness, accusations and judgments, which always helps. What needs to be addressed becomes the underlying dynamic, usually hidden, for the imbalance in the first place, not the behaviour itself. Just as in Naturopathic medicine, you do not treat the skin rash directly, but more the hidden underlying organic weakness that has led to it; which, in turn, is related to eating and sleeping habits that also need to be addressed.

When everything happening is seen as a manifestation of love at work, even when it does not look like it, a couple become co-detectives trying to work out together what is needed. They explore the *relationship* rather than each other, which is a lot less confrontational and divisive. Coming together to learn from love immediately shifts perspective away from blame, judgment and mutual recrimination. It reconnects the partners with the real reason they are together in the first place, which is that they love each other. The conflicts become food for love rather than frightening events that threaten the life of the relationship. The inevitable struggles and fights are seen as having meaning rather than signs that something is wrong. Problems and difficulties, because they are not so threatening, are dealt with sooner, before they grow into great divides. This all creates a very different context for partners to communicate and understand each other.

Each relationship has a unique combination of these different aspects of love. This combination will change overtime. As a result, what a relationship needs will also change. What is needed when you are first together is very different from what you need when you have children, which is different again from what you need at retirement. An understanding of this transcendental, overarching dimension to love will support your relationship and offer help at every stage of the journey. This is because the most reliable and most closely attuned source of guidance will always be your own love.

CHAPTER FOUR

Across the Great Divide

The minute I heard my first love story
I started looking for you, not knowing
how blind that was.
Lovers don't finally meet somewhere.
They're in each other all along.
RUMI

Being guided by love sounds like a good idea, but how do we do it? 'Linking' is a set of processes and techniques that help you link into and learn about your love. The idea is that you link into and access the third force of all relationships, the body of the relationship, which in loving relationships is the body of your love. One core process involves you sitting together and talking to your love, rather than directly to each other. Instead of facing each other from opposite sides of the negotiating table, you sit side by side, looking at the situation from the same viewpoint. This process, especially useful in conflicts, achieves several objects:

- It defuses some of the antagonism and confrontation that more easily surface when facing each other.
- You are reminded that you are in this together, and that to move forward requires the involvement of both of you.
- It brings the relationship into play and asks the relationship to get involved in sorting out what needs to be understood and done. And the body of the relationship is greater than the sum of its parts.
- It re-creates a conscious connection with your love, which may have got a bit lost along the way.
- It reminds you of an aspect easily forgotten in the intensity of intimacy, which is that you are creating something together.
- It gives you the chance to receive some insight and wisdom into your situation, but from your love rather than your anxieties, hurts, angers and fears.

The way it works is simple. You sit side by side and imagine your relationship or your love on a chair facing you. To begin with, this process is more of the imagination but as the process becomes more familiar it also becomes more real. You begin to speak to your love about whatever is important to you, communicating not to each other but to the relationship or love in front of you. You refer to each other by name or 'he' or 'she', not 'you'. There are no rules for how to express yourself. You do not have to take responsibility, listen, be sensitive or empathic, be clear, say exactly what you mean or reveal anything particular. Both of you are completely free to say whatever you wish to your love. The love will take care of what is important.

Our primary struggle is often not with our partners, but with the demands and responsibilities of love

Linking is a powerful process, very different from looking at the two individuals and their interactions, as the relationship is seen as a whole, as a single body. One of the effects of this process is a natural and organic unravelling of any tangle and struggle between you. The struggle becomes one you are both having with your love, and this is closer to the truth than that you are struggling with each other.

In Linking exercises, all that is needed is the truth. As you share whatever is there, this simple honesty will always take you on to the next step in the exploration. If you are not willing to reveal yourself, you can always say: 'I do not want to share myself. And as this is the truth, the next step will be revealed and the process will unfold all the same. Whatever the love of the relationship needs will become clear through this exercise. Though whether you choose to pay attention or not is up to you.

Let us look at how this works with a specific example.

> *A man and a woman had been together for many years. They had worked hard creating a home and bringing up their children who were now grown up. He began an affair with a younger woman he met at work. The wife discovered his affair and when she confronted her husband he confessed all. He had been involved with this other woman for two years. They came to couples' counselling with their relationship in crisis.*

Love is more than a feeling, it is a state of being

In this situation one of the first priorities is to find out whether the individuals still love each other or not. This is different from whether they want to stay together. The woman may want the man to stop his affair and remain faithful to her because she cannot face making public their estrangement, though she may no longer love him. Or the man may feel so burdened with guilt, or may feel the shame and turmoil of breaking up would be too much for him, that he would choose to end the affair even though he no longer loves his wife. But both these options will lead eventually to even deeper trouble, simply because a love that is not evolving into greater creativity is devolving into greater destructivity. This is a topic we return to later.

When love has died between a couple then usually a good funeral is the best option, a goodbye that celebrates the life that has been lived, the love that there has been. It is possible for a couple to separate with their love intact because the relationship has changed and they need to move on, but there is always some grieving to be gone through for what has gone. And, of course, if one partner needs to move on, so does the other, though they may not realise this for some time. Why would anyone need or want to stay with someone who is no longer in love with them, when it is so painful to live like this? Only if they are so familiar with being rejected, kept at a distance or unloved, that the alternative, being alone, seems worse. In which case, being alone for a while may banish that fear and lead to a deeper healing than would otherwise happen if they stayed together. Love is still at work even when a relationship ends. Love will always seek new forms in which to express itself and will sometimes cause a person to leave a relationship in order to remain alive in that person's life. Staying can sometimes be more harmful to love than leaving. We will go into all this later; we are merely introducing some of these ideas at this point.

No-one other than the couple concerned knows the truth about whether they love each other or not. The couple always knows, though neither may admit it, even to themselves. If you sit side by side with your partner facing the body of your love on an empty chair in front of you, you will know the truth about whether you love each other or not. You may be too afraid to admit it, even to yourself, but you will both know. Maybe you feel anxious or afraid that your partner no longer loves you, or shame that you no longer love them in the way you once did, and these feelings make it hard to face up to the reality. Or you may feel nothing, a kind of depression, an alienation, a flatness that is hard to define or articulate. Or you may feel so angry that you can feel no love whatsoever, yet underneath the anger you are very much in love. Our feelings are not the best guide for whether we are in love or not. Love is more than a feeling – it is a state of being.

Being in love with someone is different from simply loving them

You can love someone but not want to make love with them. Loving someone means you have welcomed them into your heart and let them live there, but it does not necessarily involve a physical intimacy. In sexual love, however, we are literally making love, creating a body of love that grows to surround us. This love can then become available for many other aspects of life, especially for any children that may result, but sexual love is the crucible in which it is made. Living in this love is being in love. A couple may begin making this love through their sexual intimacy and create a body of love that is then fed through their emotional intimacy, but it originates in the sexuality of their love.

If a couple stay together when they are no longer making love, either physically through sexual intimacy or emotionally through an intimacy of their inner experience, then slowly they will fall out of being in love though they may still love each other. They may continue to live together in a comfort and familiarity they both value. Then again, they may decide to move on. This may not be a conscious choice. One or other may simply find themselves falling in love with someone else without any conscious intent. The sexual instincts, like all life, will seek to remain alive and can find someone to make love with, whether the person is conscious of this process or not. That this happens is simply life trying to bring about its continued incarnation through the sexual instincts, an 'expression of life's longing for itself', and is not really in the realm of choice at all. The freedom lies in what we decide to do.

Instinct, not knowledge, reveals the ways of love

The love-body of a relationship is of energy and is therefore experienced through our energy and feeling rather than our intellects. One way to attune to love is through the way our bodies relate with our partner – the body language, the unconscious shifts in posture, the way we sit, eye movements, tone of voice, and so on. Another way is through our actual *behaviour* – what we actually *do* rather than what we say. In the case described above, if the man is saying he wants to rebuild the relationship with his wife but is continuing to meet the other woman, what he is actually *doing* is a truer reflection of his energy than his stated intentions. Or if the woman says she loves her husband yet attacks him every time he approaches her, then her actions are indicating a different reality from her statements of loving him. To attack him some of the time, even most of the time, while she is feeling so hurt and angry, is natural, but not *every* time. But by far the most important way to attune to the energy of love is to pay attention to the sensations in our own bodies.

The instinctual knowledge lying in the subtle sensations within our bodies can give us information about the energy of situations long before they are revealed externally in behaviour or words. Even deciphering the meaning of behaviour and body language requires us to think, whereas our feelings and instincts can sense immediately a level of reality not available to more conscious modes of analysis. Other animals, using these same instincts, will often sense events long before we do. We used to live in the middle of a forest that was devastated by a hurricane. Three days before the storm, which human weather forecasters categorically denied was coming, all the deer, birds and animals that lived there simply left. No-one knew where they had gone. Three nights later the storm came and uprooted and felled most of the trees. The next day the animals began to return, again following their instincts.

Attuning to your instincts and the hidden levels of what is going on involves actively listening to the subtle feelings and sensations within our own bodies, which most of us have learned to ignore or control rather than pay attention to. I will go into all this in later chapters.

Our relationships are our teachers and guides into the ways of love

Let us return to the example of the couple struggling to save their relationship from the fallout after an affair.

This couple clearly loved each other and, although there was much ambivalence, they wanted their relationship to work, though did not know what to do. However, when the man made a move towards her, the woman often rejected him with anger and bitterness at the betrayal she felt. She was so hurt and wounded that her rage and hurt flared up continually. The man withdrew from these attacks and withdrew into himself. The situation was critical.

Neither could change how they felt, or stop their reactions to each other, despite both wanting something more productive to happen. This dynamic had to be released in order for love to begin flowing again. I suggested they tap into a greater power than their own selves – their love.

The couple sat together on a sofa and imagined the body of their relationship facing them. They began to speak to their relationship. The man spoke first and, without the immediate attacks from his hurt wife, he began to speak about how guilty, powerless and hopeless he felt. When the woman spoke to the relationship-body, she focused less on her husband and connected more directly with herself. She talked about how she hated feeling so hurt and angry.

One aspect of the struggle with love that emerges in all intimate sexual relationships is that love keeps trying to teach us how to love, and we don't realise how much we have to learn. We think we know how to love, but there are depths and dimensions to love far beyond what we know or can even imagine, and love keeps trying to teach us these deeper truths. Another aspect of our struggle with love, which we all engage in until we don't, is that love makes demands of us to let go the defensive positions of our egos and discover the realities of life beyond our fear. And we resist this. Many struggles between partners are really each one's struggle with the demands of love rather than with each other. But more about this later.

Once he no longer needed to defend himself from direct attack, the man began to feel how underneath his guilt there was a deep hurt and sadness. The woman heard him speak of this and became even more angry at what she described as his selfishness and lack of sensitivity – why should he feel so hurt, when it was he that had betrayed her, not the other way around?

Love can transform struggle, confusion and pain into more love

The situation between the couple in crisis remained critical, but rather than making the woman work through *her* process and the man *his*, Linking focuses on the *relationship*. The body of love in the relationship needed to be healed and supported if the couple were to begin to build their lives together again. To focus on the relationship we first need to take the pressure off the two individuals to change. This reduces whatever pressure they put on themselves to somehow sort it out, explain themselves, be more loving, get it together, be reasonable, listen, not be so angry, and be patient, whatever.

It helps to recognise that neither partner can really help what they are doing and feeling, and besides, it is likely that if they could do it differently, they would. However, the Linking process would say there is no need to be doing it differently anyway. Love is operating according to a deeper wisdom than we can ever fully know. The only option is to switch focus away from the anger and pain, tap back into the love directly, then bring all the anger, pain, frustration, grief and fear to the love. Again and again I have witnessed in my personal life and my work as a relationship counsellor that when partners simply lay everything they think and feel at the feet of the relationship – their contradictory hopes and fears, resentments and appreciations, hostilities and love – then something profoundly revealing and healing happens. There is nothing that we need to do other than be as honest as we can be with all the different aspects of ourselves. By simply bringing ourselves to the relationship, love transforms the situation. And what is more, it only requires one of a couple to do this.

In my experience, in most relationships if one partner sincerely turns to love for help, then the other responds, even if they are not present. A genuine turning to your love means you are open to something other than your previously polarised position, which encourages your partner to correspondingly move.

Love always makes us vulnerable to heartbreak

Asking our love to work for us does not mean we develop a detached, non-emotional way of relating that protects us from the vulnerability of loving. On the contrary, the more we develop a relationship with our love, the more we realise not only its power but also its vulnerability. A relationship can be destroyed and killed just as can a plant, a species of bird, an enemy, a habitat, a person or the spirit of a child. All these can die, and so can love in a particular form. Love may be eternal in some aspects, but in the form of a particular relationship, love can die. Yet we are usually more aware of our own vulnerability to love than love's vulnerability to us.

To dare to love someone is to be vulnerable to them – we are 'able to be wounded'. Because we naturally fear this, we develop defences that protect us by reducing the power of love over us. Without meaning to, we diminish our capacity for loving and being loved, in order to save ourselves from heartbreak. In a variety of ways we reject, attack, undermine, ignore or run away from love, usually without knowing what we are doing – that is, until we realise that when we harm love there is heartbreak anyway. And often we only reach this through having our hearts broken. Ancient Chinese tradition has it that our hearts have to break seven times before we can find wisdom. That's a lot of love needed before we become wise.

There is always an equality in a relationship, though this is often hidden

Linking helps develop an understanding that is neither judgmental nor prescriptive and involves, amongst other techniques, exploring the history of the relationship, not merely the separate histories of the two individuals. When exploring the relationship, themes emerge that have usually been present from the very beginning. Difficulties that may manifest themselves 20 or 30 years later were usually present in some form or other from the time the couple fell in love. In fact, it is usually the very aspects of each other that initially attracted the couple that are later at the root of the deepest trouble.

One of the principles behind the way loving relationships work is that whatever dynamic can be seen operating from one person to the other will have a similar dynamic (though this is usually hidden) working the other way. So, whenever there is a direct accusation, such as in this example, where the woman says that the man has betrayed her but she has not betrayed him, the Linking process takes a deeper look. In what way might the woman have betrayed their love? In the exploration of their history together this is likely to come to light. It may be that there were repeated small betrayals of love on a daily basis. It may have been something that happened periodically, for example he might have on occasions tried to talk with her about being unhappy at work but because he was earning such a good salary, the wife ignored his need and would not discuss this. This is also a betrayal of their love. Or an exact equivalent may be found some time in the past. If you look deeply enough, this is what you will usually find, a hidden reciprocity or symmetry – in this case, a more intimate betrayal.

> *It emerged that for the first two years of their marriage the woman had been closer and more intimate with her mother than with her husband. She had revealed private aspects of their life together to this third party, telling secrets that he gave her for safe-keeping and revealing intimate details of their sex life. The level at which this hurt him had been buried because he did not know why he had felt so abandoned and betrayed. He had judged it as inadequate or irrational to feel this way, and when he tried to talk with her about his distress, she had defended herself and told him he was being controlling and possessive. The wound could not be dealt with as both were in their different ways ignoring it. It then went underground where it lay neglected and unattended for many years.*

This much later affair was not a conscious attempt on the man's part to put the relationship to rights, but it could be seen as love's way of bringing to the surface a deep wound that had never healed and which needed to be addressed for their love to grow. There was the potential at this point in their lives, now the children had grown, for deeper intimacy between them, and their love was doing all it could to bring about the right conditions for this. Freed from the demands of parenthood there was also more emotional energy available for the relationship, which would be needed to digest all this from their past. Love had chosen its time well.

Both partners are equally responsible for the love in a relationship

By bringing this reciprocity to light, the couple could begin to move into balance again. This is a complex process that I will describe in detail later, but one of the key things here was that they began to acknowledge that *both* had played a part in what had happened. Neither was therefore the victim of the other. This is extremely important. By each taking responsibility for what happens in a relationship, a couple is no longer divided. They can no longer simply blame each other and can become instead co-detectives uncovering together the source of their difficulties. By taking responsibility for what is happening you stop trying to change your partner, and there is relief all round at this. However, in a traumatic relationship, you might decide to change your situation instead and leave.

I have often observed when working with couples that both will take a deep breath, a sort of sigh of relief, which neither may notice, at exactly the moment they recognise a reciprocity in the relationship. It is as if the body of the relationship relaxes and both feel immediately safer and more at ease.

Love may be at work even when we feel anything but loving

As soon as we acknowledge that the relationship and the love have been created equally by both partners, something new can begin to reveal itself. In this example, even if the woman continues to think what he did to her was worse than anything she did to him, her body has already begun to relax and absorb the deeper reality. The woman may well feel compelled to keep punishing the man, resisting his overtures, lashing out at him and refusing to open up to him. But once they have acknowledged their love for each other and each has taken responsibility for the relationship, this can be seen as love operating again to bring their relating back into a healthy balance by balancing out the hurt. As an old proverb tells us: 'If you would forgive your enemy, first you must wound him'.

This symmetrical wounding, which may look like revenge, is not necessarily harmful. It is happening for reasons we may not be able to see. Yet knowing that love is at work, even when it doesn't look like what we have been taught is loving, means we will stop interfering with its workings by imposing our ideas of what should be happening – for instance, that the woman should forgive and forget, or that she should never forgive and forget and should leave. It may be that without her attacks, the woman would never be able to open up to her husband again, and this would leave her with no option other than leaving or spending the rest of her life unable to make love with him. When the hurt has been at such a deep instinctual level, our instincts are usually a far better guide as to what is needed than our intellects.

> *The man and the woman began to build their life together again. It was often difficult but there were also moments when they were closer than they had ever been. Sometimes it felt like when they first met. What also happened was that many other aspects of their relationship became clearer and more harmonious, without them doing anything particular to address them. He began to buy her presents and he had not done that for a very long time. She began to cook wonderful meals*

for them both and she had not done that for a very long time either. They went to the theatre, out to dinner and on holidays together, all aspects of their life that had been lost for some time (romantic love had been a large part of their loving). Love began again to work its magic between them.

When love is greater than fear, it naturally continues to extend itself

When the love between a couple grows to include more and more of each other, then whatever happens between them takes place *within* the love. The love is then greater than whatever anger, fear, pain, feelings of betrayal, guilt, hatred, shame or desire to punish or run away might be going on. This means that alongside resentments, anger and pain there is also room for other things, such as understanding, laughter, vulnerability, self-revelation, forgiveness and closeness. But these other possibilities enter the picture in a natural and organic way, not because they are forced or imposed. Eventually there is the space for everything in the love. And when everything is in love, an even deeper magic can begin.

In this case the man began to understand that his wife had to periodically attack him – it was love's way through her of bringing their relationship into balance. Because of the depth of their denial about the earlier hurt, this crisis had to emerge in a very flamboyant form to bring attention to the hidden wound. He also felt less guilty about his affair, which, contrary to many people's intuitive sense that it is right to feel guilty about these things, was helpful. He was more willing to engage with his wife when he no longer felt he had to defend himself. She felt his presence in the relationship more and as a result felt safer and able to share her underlying hurt and vulnerability more easily. This brought them closer, and what had been a spiral into deeper alienation and misunderstanding became a movement towards more intimacy and trust.

They also began to value their love as an intricate and subtle source of wisdom in their lives. With their renewed connection with their love, this couple also reached out and became available to their children in a new way, and their love not only nourished their own relationship, it became a source of support to others, too.

The 10 steps of Linking into the relationship when love is in crisis

The Linking process described in this example involves the following steps:

1   An exploration of the love in the relationship, the degree to which the love-body is out of balance or even alive. This is an energetic process, not an intellectual or verbal exercise – a kind of diagnosis. The two individuals always know the state of their love, though may not admit it, even to themselves.

2 A shift of perspective away from seeing what is happening as being between the two people to one of focusing on the relationship and the body of love.

3 Bringing together the separate individuals to explore side by side their relationship and their love.

4 Taking the pressure off the individuals to change.

5 Expressing freely to the body of the relationship without any rules as to what to say or how to say it.

6 Exploring the history of the relationship.

7 Finding the key areas of imbalance.

8 Understanding the meaning of what has happened/is happening rather than judging it as right or wrong.

9 Each recognising the relationship is a creation of them both, and that both are therefore responsible for the imbalance and the rebalancing.

10 Trusting love again. Which is not the same as trusting the other person.

Fear of love is in all of us, in some form or other

Trusting love is not easy. Most of us know that love can lead to heartbreak, and so to some degree are naturally afraid of this. The fear may show itself in different ways. Some, for example, may shy away from commitment, while others may demand too much commitment. Both ways, though, avoid the real vulnerability of loving and being loved. We have therefore developed a variety of ways to protect ourselves from love. Some we have learned from our parents, school and friends, and from the cultural climate around us; some we have uniquely designed and created ourselves. However we acquired them, every tactic we have created to avoid being hurt by love will be triggered in intimate sexual relationships. When our partner challenges the ways in which we are avoiding the vulnerability of love (and they will!), this is love's way of teaching us, through the relationship, how to love wholeheartedly again. Similarly, we will challenge our partners. In the heat of a fight, however, we are unlikely to be open and available to learn from love. And, anyway, it can be more important to have the fight, releasing tension and pent-up feelings, then later in a cooler climate learn from it. We will go into all this in greater detail later.

However fearful we may be of the potential woundings of intimacy, of our partner rejecting us, of being overwhelmed by demands, of being abandoned or used, or whatever is our fear (and we all have many of these!), our love is not a force that will ever actually harm us. Love does not, for example, ever interfere with our freedom, undermine our authority, control our spontaneity, limit our self-expression or in any other way prevent us from having what we need. Neither does it judge us, frighten us, reject us, attack us or bully us. Love simply does not do these things – fear might, but not love. Linking into our love helps us trust the process of relationship, even when we cannot trust our partner. And we cannot always trust them as they do not always know what is going on any more than we do. Yet we can always trust love.

Love can bring into our life everything we need if we let it

Linking works on many levels:

- It brings you together on the same side, not as enemies opposing each other.
- It empowers each in the recognition that both have created the situation.
- It stops blame and righteous judgments.
- It unlocks the conflict from the polarised positions it has assumed.
- It opens up deeper levels of what is really going on.
- It provides a safe place where you can explore these levels.
- It does not interfere or harm your relationship because it *is* the relationship.
- It feeds your relationship by bringing you into alignment with the reason you are together in the first place, because you love each other even when you don't feel it.
- It helps you trust love again.

Linking is useful for many other purposes, not only when a relationship is in difficulty. Learning to use the energy of your love to create understanding, happiness, healing, insight, pleasure and more love is the most powerful process many people have found, not only for their relationship, but in the creation of a good life on every level. This does not mean love is the ultimate consumer dream. It means that love will bring into our life what our love needs, such as a home close to nature, work that is fulfilling spiritually and emotionally, happy children, and a beautiful and safe environment.

We tend to think in our advanced capitalist society that only money can give us these things, and so suffer in the pursuit of financial wealth, forgetting the wealth that love can bring. We have lost the art of using the power of love to create the good life for ourselves and our children. One way to rediscover it is to sit in front of the body of your love and simply lay all your concerns, hopes, worries, feelings, thoughts and beliefs at the feet of your love. Let it simply lie there, in front of your love, while you do nothing but wait. You can do this together side by side, with your partner or alone. Something will always happen. Slowly it begins to dawn on you that you have tapped into a primal source of magic that has a power beyond what we can ever understand. All I can say is try it and see for yourself.

Some couples who work together have special business meetings where anything and everything is spoken to the relationship-body, and through this process it gradually becomes clear what needs to be done. Others have regular times when they share anything they want to with the body of their love, as a routine that supports the on-going challenges of living together, creating a home, caring for children, managing finances, and so on. Out of this process decisions emerge naturally, rather like what once may have happened in tribal meetings where elders spoke until the right course of action revealed itself. We may have lost this facility in our modern communities, but it is absolutely possible in our families.

When the love between sexually intimate partners grows, this body of love becomes the energy field within which both live. They live in love, but a love that is inclusive not exclusive, as it continually grows to embrace more and more of life. Anyone who comes into the energy field of such a love is affected by it and receives some benefit, especially, of course, their children.

For the couple themselves there is a deeper goodness. When with the one you love and who loves you in this complete way, frustrations at work, the loss of a friend, moving house, financial trouble, storms at sea and even death have a goodness in them, too. This is because such a love is a greater force than even death. And as the old Apache song says, 'Around it everything is beautiful.'

CHAPTER FIVE

One Plus One Equals Three

Your father and mother were playing love games.
They came together and you appeared!
Don't ask what love can do!
Look at the colours of the world.
RUMI

The whole is greater than the sum of its parts

There is a strange force at work in intimate sexual relationships. It cannot be explained using psychological ideas or explanations that see human relationships primarily in terms of interactions between individuals. Yet most descriptions of human relationships are in these terms. It is rather like trying to understand the behaviour of a flock of birds by examining the individual birds and seeing how they affect or communicate with one another. Biologists and ethologists tried for many years to analyse the movement of birds but it was only when they looked at the flock as a single living entity, rather than as a collection of individual birds, that they could understand the flight patterns. Swarms of insects, schools of fish, herds of cattle, groups of gorillas, and families of animals everywhere are being understood in new ways by examining them systemically as whole bodies rather than as collections of individual bodies. Yet we are only beginning to apply this to human relationships.

The psychology of the individual has been studied in depth, but an understanding of the parts can never explain the whole. As a consequence, we do not yet have a scientific explanation of what goes on in families, groups and in the heart of intimate relationships. Which is why we call it a 'strange' force – because we have yet to explain what is happening with our analytical minds. Our instincts and intuition, operating through sensation and feeling, on the other hand, understand very well. This is because the strange force is love.

Falling in love is a matter of instinct and feeling not thought

When I describe love as a force field or energy-body, I am describing what I have observed and experienced in my own relationship and in the relationships of friends, family and the couples I have worked with over the last 30 years. I don't really know *why* what I have observed happens in any scientific sense, but the more I have engaged in an exploration of love, the more I have learned to trust my instincts and intuitions. And if you think about it, that is what we all do anyway.

Falling in love in the first place is a matter of instinct and feeling rather than rational thought. Our check lists of what we want in a partner go out the window when we find ourselves sexually attracted to someone who, for some reason we cannot explain, we feel drawn to. We might have had fantasies of a tall, dark, rich stranger only to find ourselves attracted to a smaller, fair, poorer, old friend who suddenly appears to us in a different light – as a sexual partner. What do we do? Do we reject the possibility because this person does not meet our criterion, as we would a car with no sunroof, or a flat with too small a balcony, or do we follow our instincts? Most of us will follow the older, some might say wiser, animal instincts of the body.

A woman and a man had been together for nine years. Their relationship had been intense, with both passion and love as well as deep struggle and fights. Eventually their fights became so painful they separated. Contact was difficult between them after this and in order to let go of each other and create new lives, they decided to cut all ties. The man went to live in another country. This was particularly painful for the woman, as the separation had been at the instigation of the man. They were apart for two years and during that time they had no communication and both had other lovers.

Unusually, one day she travelled to work by bus. On her way home she saw someone standing ready to get off who looked very like her old partner. She then noticed the shoes he was wearing and recognised them. She had helped him choose them. It was her old partner. He was in England for a few days visiting his parents and had come to the city she lived in to see his dentist. They had lunch together.

Their connection was so deep, however, that after a few meetings it became clear that they must either get back together again or stop trying to be friends and leave each other's lives completely. The woman did not know which was right. The man decided it would be better to say goodbye. His grandfather had left his grandmother only to return and a few years later, become seriously ill and die. His father had left his mother and returned only when he was too ill to make his own life. The man could not face a repeat of this scenario. So they thanked each other for the love there had been, wished each other well and said goodbye.

> *Later that evening the man called the woman. In the way she had said goodbye with love, he felt she had found herself in a new way and he realised that he loved her and wanted to be with her. The woman was more cautious. The next evening they met. The woman did not know what to do, and the only way that occurred to her to find out was that they go to bed together and see what happened. They discovered that they loved each other and in some way they could not explain were meant to be together. However, the woman was not pleased. She had been having fantasies of a relationship with a very different person from this man, and she knew how difficult this one was. In her fantasies her next partner would be someone with whom life would be harmonious and peaceful. But this was not to be. This man was the one. Love had arranged things differently from her plans.*

We find our mates, as do other animals, through our sexual instincts, through the energetic processes of the body. Since the body is the seat of the unconscious, there are many more parts of us involved when we fall in love than we know about consciously. It is interesting that in what is probably one of the most important decisions of our life, we rely on our reptilian lower brain stem and mammalian instincts more than our celebrated cerebral cortex and thought. But then it is through the body that we come into life and without it we would not be interested in sexual love at all.

Arranged marriages are a different matter. These can fulfill many functions. They can create useful alliances between families, protect families from harm, and restore peace between warring tribes. They can also lead to sexual love and passion, but this is not their primary goal. The primary goal is connected with what the *families* need, simply because it is the families that make the choice. These days, however, knowing there will be trouble otherwise, the individual's wishes are generally respected as well, even in cultures with a long tradition of arranged marriages. Love operates its profound mysteries through families, too, but in advanced capitalist societies we emphasise the rights and freedom of the individual more than our belonging to family and community, and as a result we choose our own mates in our own individual way. It is these freely chosen relationships that are being referred to here.

The way we fall in love reverberates through the life of the relationship

There are many ways of falling in love, just as there are many ways of making it. Your eyes might meet across a crowded room and there is love at first sight. Or there may be a dawning realisation that the friend you have worked with for the last two years is actually someone you love. Or it might be you are shocked into a recognition that you are in love when your partner leaves because they felt you did not love them enough. The way a couple fall in love reverberates in different ways throughout the life of the relationship, rather like a seed contains within it a blueprint for the whole plant. The repeating cycle of that first falling in love seems to continually invite us to fall in love all over again.

Even when both partners are turning their backs on love, love will call out to us, trying to remind us of a deeper reality than our anxieties and frustrations remember. Sometimes we don't hear until something dramatic happens. We forget a birthday, are late for an important event for our partner, our partner screams at us, there is a terrible row in the car over map-reading, a precious object is broken, and so on. If we do not pay attention to this, then an even deeper call is sent out – there is an accident, an affair, a depression, and so on. When the tide of love has gone a long way out, then often the turn happens through a similar process that brought the two together in the first place.

> A woman met a man at her work and slowly fell in love with him, yet he didn't seem interested in her. After a year of pining quietly she decided to invite him for dinner and told him how she felt. He was shocked and had genuinely no idea she had felt this way. He told her he was still in love with an old girlfriend who had moved to another city, though they were not seeing very much of each other and she now seemed more interested in her life there than in him. The woman decided she had to let go and move on. This was difficult because of her job, but she quit and found work elsewhere.
>
> After their conversation the man realised how much he had been holding on to a relationship that was no longer alive or going anywhere. He realised he had to move on from his old love and let her go. Having created a space inside himself, he then realised how much he was missing the companionship of the woman who had left. He actually missed her so much that suddenly it struck him how exceptionally attractive, intelligent and funny she was, and that he wanted her. He tracked her down and told her his feelings, putting his heart at her feet. They began a relationship. Eventually they married.
>
> Throughout their long and, at times, tumultuous relationship there would be a repeat of this pattern. The woman would feel things

going on and wanted to explore them with him, but she could not get through to him. Because he did not respond she would assume he was not interested, and after trying everything she could she would give up and walk away. Each time after she had gone the shock had such a dramatic effect upon the man that he realised, through the experience of having her gone, how important she was to him. He would find her, even if this time only in the next bedroom, and tell her how sorry he was and that he had not realised he was putting something relatively unimportant before their relationship. So genuine was his love for her that this process would transform him and whatever had been the specific difficulty was, each time, never a problem again. She would then open up to him and they would begin another phase of their lives together.

This repeated cycle, similar to how their relationship began, taught them many things. He learned not to let his desire for success lead him to ignore matters at home, to share his worries and not to pretend always to be OK, and not to keep important secrets from her. Each time he learned that their love mattered more to him than whatever else he was putting first. Meanwhile, she was learning each time to return to herself rather than looking solely to the relationship for what she needed. He began to trust the relationship while she began to trust herself.

They realised that though she turned first to the relationship and only later to herself, he would first try to deal with things alone and only later turn to the relationship. They also realised they learned about their relationship in different ways, she through communication and insight, he through direct experience. This is why her many attempts to talk with him failed but her actions never did. These differences, the source of many fights, were also the source of much pleasure and fun, and a major part of why their lives worked so well together.

Everything that happens in a relationship can be used to make love

Blaming each other for difficulties never works. And anyway, when looking for the meaning of behaviour, rather than condemning it, judgments about what is good or bad, right or wrong, change. A couple will often say to each other, after having worked through issues that have emerged as a consequence of some apparently unfortunate event or some difficulty between them, how lucky it was that this seemingly bad thing had happened. An affair can lead to a renewed intimacy within the relationship as the individuals are forced to deal with issues between them that they had ignored. A redundancy can lead to a revitalising of the relationship rather than a slow stagnation from a routine that was not challenged. Many times relationship counsellors hear how couples are grateful that a crisis forced them to re-engage with each other and rediscover their love. Yet this challenge is around most of the time, if not all of the time. Even what we initially condemn can be made into love in our intimate relationships.

Love's alchemy can turn base metal into gold. No money for one person can seem a tragedy, but for another a new freedom; a broken leg can mean a frustrating break from work, but also time to reflect on things. It is the meaning we give events that is significant – our relationship with what happens, rather than events per se. This is why when we begin to tap into another dimension of love, 'good' and 'bad' take on different meanings. Once we know love is at work, we naturally want to find out what something means, what is the context which gave rise to it, what are the forces this is trying to rebalance, and where are the hidden symmetries. This leads to a very different exploration than one where something is judged as wrong and must therefore be changed.

> *A woman came to counselling. She wanted to give up smoking and had tried many times, using many methods. Her partner hated her smoking, both because of the smell and the worry for her health and the health of their children. In desperation she came to counselling to see if there were psychological ways that might help her. She confessed that she was not honest with her partner about how much she really smoked, chewing mints to disguise the smell, hiding cigarette packets and secreting ashtrays in cupboards. She felt very unhappy and guilty about this deception, as in other areas of the relationship there was an honesty and intimacy that was very important to them both. This issue was clearly affecting their relationship more than might initially have been apparent. Instead of pursuing the emotional and psychological reasons for her smoking – childhood loss, anxiety, hidden depressions – I suggested we use the higher power of their relationship to help her. And anyway, if she could have given up under her own steam she would have already done so.*
>
> *She brought her partner with her to the next session. He clearly thought it was her lack of willpower that was the problem but decided*

it was worth a try. They began a Linking process to call on the body of their love to help them. Immediately there was a relief in her as they sat side by side looking at the smoking together, allies rather than adversaries. He reached out to take her hand and she began to cry. She spoke about how she had felt so bad, so guilty and ashamed. He was shocked by how distressed she was, and explained how he only wanted the best for her and their children. This had been his intention, not to hurt or condemn her. They decided to spend some time each day, sitting together, on the same side of the table, looking at the smoking as a problem they were both faced with and both would be needed to solve.

It emerged that his decision to work with her rather than leaving her to cope alone had a powerful impact. She had always felt she would only be loved when she was giving something. That he was willing to involve himself in something she had felt so ashamed of, for no other reason than that he cared for her, touched her deeply. He, on the other hand, was so affected by the depth of her feelings of not being loved that he ceased completely to condemn her smoking and instead told her it mattered more to him that she felt loved than that she stopped smoking. She began to feel, in a new way, how much he loved her. Their increased emotional closeness led him to talk about himself more deeply than before – how he did what he thought was right rather than what he felt, how it was hard for him to express his love for her and their children, and that he hadn't even realised how important this was. His fierce judgments of her smoking were reflected as deeply, if not more, in his buried judgments of himself, and this was the other face of his integrity that had attracted her to him in the first place. More and more surfaced simply as a result of their sitting together to deal with the problem. And whether the smoking stopped or not became less important to both of them. The smoking could stop in its time as there was now no need to force anything. Their redemptive love for each other's hidden pain had come into play. They could relax and let love do the work.

Here we can see how immediately the love in a relationship can work, once we have invited it to. Had we gone into her hidden shame and guilt and feelings of unworthiness within traditional therapy, then this process, although helpful and healing, could have taken years. Sitting with her partner, it all happened spontaneously (plus saving a lot in therapist's fees!).

The emotional intimacy of sexual love has the potential for deep healing

The transference between client and therapist, the bonding between them without which therapeutic exploration cannot go deep, can take a long time to achieve. And even then it is nowhere near the potent intimacy we have with our lovers. The emotional intimacy created by sharing our inner worlds with our sexual partners is, however, a relatively new phenomenon. For most of human history, family relationships have been more pragmatic, cemented around the process of creating a home, having children, working and surviving. A familiarity grew that was unspoken. Emotional intimacy is now, however, a vital part of our sexual relationships and marriage. The sharing of secret hopes and fears has become the currency of modern love, which makes the healing and redemptive powers of sexual love very potent.

Early psychoanalysts were the first to encourage people to voice their hidden thoughts and feelings and to give them a meaning. Prior to this, shameful secrets were revealed only in the confessional to be forgiven, not to be understood or analysed. Freud found that when someone was encouraged to speak freely of their inner world without censorship, a deep bond was created between the one speaking and the one listening. This bonding awoke the long-forgotten passions and struggles of early childhood when this same level of bond existed between a child and its parents. The basic theme of psychotherapy is that the intense feelings of early childhood return and are transferred to the therapist, who becomes a parent figure. Unresolved conflicts are re-experienced with the therapist and released, freeing us from being controlled unconsciously by our past.

These deep bondings, however, no longer occur in the confessional or on the analyst's couch, but in bed with our sexual partners. The healing and freedom between partners in a committed love relationship is therefore potentially the deepest. Not only is the bonding so intense, but it intimately involves the body. Lying in our partner's arms, sharing secrets, feeling ourselves in new ways as we emotionally and physically let go, deepens the bonding. Making love literally makes us love each other. It can also heal emotional wounds as forgotten feelings and memories come to the surface and are released, in ways that reach parts no therapy can. The energy field of the love can eventually become so powerful that by simply being in the love, in love, we are healed and released from past hurts together without needing to do or say anything. But it takes a lot of love for this.

Our love can become a greater force than our fear

A monastery in Thailand that cures people addicted to drugs has the lowest rate of relapse in the world. People have gone many times to see how they achieve this, hoping to emulate it in their own countries, but no-one has yet succeeded. The treatment consists of giving each person a simple monk's cell and leaving them alone apart from taking care of them physically and feeding them. There are no special diets or medication, no individual therapy or group meetings. It seems that what cures people is the energy field of the monks. Through their meditation and commitment to the Buddhist way of life, they have created a collective force field within which the power of their presence is greater than the power of the addiction. Simply by being there the visitors attune to a force greater than their addiction and are thus released from its power over them.

In the same way, the energy field of love created by our loving can grow into a force greater than whatever keeps us away from love – our fears, desires, wills, defensiveness, etc. Eventually our love becomes so powerful that, simply by being together, everything happens that needs to.

Therapy helps us most when it supports us to create healthy, fulfilling relationships in our own life, not prolonging a dependency on the therapist or the therapeutic process. In sexual love especially, healing will penetrate not only our heart but the patterns of pain buried in the tensions in our body. Sexual love reaches parts nothing else can. It resurrects the body from the numbness, rigidity and shallow breathing that prevent us from feeling when the pain is too great, and we come back to life. And what deeper healing is there than to re-embrace life with open hearts and with the life of our own bodies.

Tuning into our love brings healing, wisdom and more love

Here are some Linking processes that help you link in with each other and your love in a new way. They can be done in a crisis, in the middle of an argument or when all is harmonious as a more general exploration. In most of the following exercises the couple sit side by side facing an empty chair. You imagine your relationship-body, or the energy field or body of your love, on the chair, either placing something there to symbolise your love or leaving it empty. You speak to this love-body, referring to each other by name and as 'she' or 'he'.

1 Talk to your love about how it feels to be sitting side by side, as if you are talking to a third person you both trust.
2 Share how you see the relationship, how you think and feel about your love.
3 Take it in turns, three minutes each, to say whatever you wish to without letting

concerns for your partner's feelings interfere with what you need or want to say. While one is speaking, the other remains silent.

4 One of you shares everything you resent about your partner, from small details (eg, they always leave their clothes lying around) to serious complaints (eg, they break their promises regularly). When they have finished the other does the same, again talking to the relationship and using the third person, not 'you'. Secondly, you repeat the process, this time sharing your hurts – again both the small hurts and the deeper wounds. Thirdly, you share your needs of your partner in the same way. This process can take as long as it needs to. Giving each stage extended time, for example 15 minutes each, means that although you may sit in silence for some time, it allows what has been buried to gradually rise to the surface.

5 In a conflict you each present your case to the body of your love, the relationship body, and keep arguing backwards and forwards three times. Then each in turn sits on the chair of the love-body and shares what you have seen from that position, as if you are speaking as the love.

6 Hold hands with your partner and both bow down to your love. Then sit in silence with your love for five to 10 minutes. Then imagine your love expanding until it surrounds you, and sit in love for another five to 10 minutes. Imagine this field of love energy expanding still further, spreading throughout the community you live in, the country, the whole planet, the solar system, the galaxy, the universe and ultimately the whole of existence. Then put on any music you like to celebrate your love.

7 When you are really up against it, face your relationship together and ask your love for help – 'Please help me', 'We need your help', 'We don't know what to do', 'I can't stand it any more, please show me the way through'. If you do this sincerely and for long enough, sitting with your love and the confusion, chaos, anger, hurt, despair and deadness, then it will change. Something will *always* happen, although the waiting can be very difficult as we naturally want quick solutions when in trouble. This exercise gives love the chance to bring something new through to the situation rather than each of you offering something only from your entrenched and polarised positions.

8 You swap roles. Each talks to the relationship body as the other might, about whatever you are exploring. You then swap back into being yourselves and again share with your love-body how you feel about what has just been said.

9 You each in turn tell the story to your relationship-body about how you met, what attracted you and how you fell in love. You then, in turn, share your disappointments with the relationship and with each other. You then turn to each

other and explore how this may be linked to whatever may be difficult in the present.

10 You each speak as you feel, to the relationship body, about what is your view of the relationship, sharing any ambivalence, uncertainties and doubts as well as your commitment, enjoyment and happiness. Now share how you feel about what you have heard expressed.

11 Each share your hopes for the relationship and then your fears. You do not have to be sensible or reasonable in what you say.

Sometimes you have to work with the love-body on your own, without your partner, perhaps because they are away, or ill, or for some reason do not want to do such exercises. The energy of your love is always present, whether or not your partner is, and the process will unfold, just the same. It can happen that one partner is more familiar with this kind of work, and without intending to uses their greater knowledge as part of a power battle going on in another area. This is natural. Relationships between the animals of this planet do not exist without periodic power battles of some form or other. However much we are convinced we are simply doing our best to work things out, when our partners refuse to work with us, it may be because we have a hidden agenda we are not aware of. If your partner does refuse, then try exploring alone. You may find that their refusal here is balanced by a different kind of refusal you give to them in another area.

We may want our partners to go in for the same kind of self-exploration we do – for example, that they read books such as this – but it may not be what is actually needed. Again and again couples have found that when one partner discovers the hidden balance, the other immediately responds even when they have not been involved in the exploration in the first place. So if your partner does not want to do these kinds of exercises, doing them alone can be just as revealing. And every sexual relationship requires both partners to have a separate life as well as a life together. The coming together would have no meaning otherwise.

CHAPTER SIX

Love's Invisible Blueprint

What is real is you and my love
for you. High in the air, unnoticed,
this reality rises into a dome
I am the Capella!
RUMI

Love organises our intimate relationships to keep them in balance

The hidden patterns and designs of intimate relationships, like the hidden patterns in nature, are not apparent until we start to look for them. Like the architecture of trees, the scales on fish, the choreography of mating rituals, the shape of a shell and the rhythm of the seasons, the patterns in loving relationships are truly amazing. In the life of a loving relationship there are remarkable synchronicities and symmetries, equivalencies and balances, events timed to perfection to bring into play what is needed at the right moment, a continuous subtle homeostasis, as if there is an overarching intelligence designing things. And the more we look for these patterns, the more we find. Here are some examples:

- An apparent strength reveals its hidden weakness in one partner at the same time as an apparent weakness in the other reveals its strength.
- A particular conflict surfaces only when there is enough love and awareness to deal with it and not before. (Whether the couple chooses to deal with it is another matter.)
- Each partner embodies for the other both their greatest hopes and their worst fears.
- What draws a couple together is precisely what will later threaten to split them apart.
- Each has exactly the energetic matrix the other needs to complete themselves.
- The balance of power is equal throughout the life of the relationship, whether the two individuals are aware of this or not.
- The way each takes care of the other is exactly what the other needs, though it may not be what they want.
- Unresolved conflicts between the parents of each repeatedly surface until they are dealt with. If repressed, they will return again in the next generation.

- The degree of vulnerability is always equal, often in very different areas, even though only one person's vulnerability may be visible.
- The power in one is precisely what will bring to the surface the vulnerability in the other.

These are some of the patterns of balance, synchronicity and symmetry that I have observed repeatedly in every sexual relationship where there is physical and emotional closeness. These patterns and others are described in greater detail in the appendix.

Like so much in the natural and physical world, when you look for these patterns, you find them. Once we know, for example, that there is likely to be a balance between the powers and vulnerabilities in each, then even when only one dimension of this is apparent, we can seek the hidden opposite and find it. Without this active investigation we might never realise there is such a balance. Yet once the buried dynamic is unearthed, we usually find it holds the key to the whole situation. There is no way all this could have been worked out consciously before the couple fell in love. So how is it that we choose a partner who manifests exactly what balances us on so many levels throughout the whole of the relationship, so that even though we can't always get what we want, we always get what we need?

What draws us to our sexual partners first is an instinctual attraction, otherwise we remain simply good friends. It seems, therefore, that the animal instincts of our bodies must have recognised the possibilities. Our instincts have a deep intelligence in these areas, just as love, too, seems to have a wisdom of its own. To bring into reality exactly what our love needs to grow is far too complex and subtle a process for our conscious minds to be able to organise. Like termites building the intricate architecture of their nests while working with an organisational complexity that rivals an army, there has to be some overarching intelligence at work, some higher power that has a greater perspective than the individuals involved. This power is the energy field of love, the love-body, which is continually creating the conditions love needs to remain alive.

When two or more gather together with a common purpose, a field of energy is created

To be able to see and appreciate love's hidden designs and magical geometry, we first need to understand more about this energy-field, this love-body, the force field of a relationship.

When people gather together in groups over time, a group body is created. Although this cannot be seen, and does not exist in material form, it is a collective energy field with a potent effect. It can be a destructive force, as in bullying gangs, lynch mobs, frenzied nationalism or religious fanaticism, or it can be creative, as in music festivals, community action, sport, therapy groups, and in the team spirit that helps people survive extreme conditions. The enlightened masters of the East used this force to help their disciples reach enlightenment in the form of the Sangha, the community that grows around a Buddha. The energy of the disciples meditating together created a collective vibration, a Buddhafield, and by meditating in this energy field the disciples were supposed to become aligned to the enlightened consciousness of the Buddha. In a very different sphere, masters of the art of war have known this, too. What wins wars is less the degree of skill of individual warriors but the team spirit of the whole army. In the business world, managers and corporations also realise that generally it is the creative dynamic between people that generates ideas, rather than individuals in their separate offices. Hence, the introduction of comfortable hanging-out areas in businesses, which encourage this coming together rather than leaving it to more erratic meetings around the photocopier.

Each collective energy field is unique, its qualities dependent on the nature of the interactions between the group members. The energy field of a therapy group, where the members are committed to listening to each other and sharing their inner worlds, is radically different from the energy field of a group where the members are committed to creating new ideas, such as a design team in manufacturing. Which is different again from local council meetings.

The level of commitment in the members is directly reflected in the nature of the group energy field. This may, of course, be nothing like what the group is saying is their commitment — a mission statement is usually created for PR purposes rather than because it is the truth. It is the energy and actual behaviour of the members that determines the group energy-field, team spirit or 'group soul'.

Love is a field of energy created by loving

When people love each other, their loving creates an energy field of love. This love-body is an inter-connectedness that transcends the individual parts. It has all the qualities of a group energy field, plus some that are uniquely the property of human sexual intimacy and love. The energy field of love created by people loving each other is what seems to be responsible for creating the patterns we observe.

This field or body of love is love. Love is not an abstract entity that vaguely dangles in the ether in some non-real existence. Like gravitational fields, electromagnetic fields, quantum matter fields in physics, and morphogenetic fields and morphic resonant fields in biology, love is a real living force, the energy field created by people loving each other. Einstein concluded: 'Reality itself is a field'. The biologist Rupert Sheldrake has suggested: 'The holistic, self-organising properties of systems at all levels of complexity, from molecules to societies, depend on such fields'. There seems to be no other way to describe how a single fertilised cell can grow according to some invisible blueprint into a living animal, or how creatures with no apparent means of communication and separated by great distances seem connected and with knowledge of each other.

Similarly, there is no other way to explain the unusual synchronicities and symmetries that occur in the life of a sexual relationship. How else is it possible for there to be a perfect mirroring in a relationship, in which what is seen in one partner is reflected back through the other? How else is it possible that the patterns of life events and experiences repeat themselves through the history of the relationship and through generations? How do events happen only when there is enough love to deal with them? How is it possible that the strengths and weaknesses of each partner are organised in ways that parallel and complement the other? And how else can the complex coordination of demands that continually challenge partners to expand their love be explained. There seems to be, in the workings of love within intimate relationships, the same overarching design or invisible blueprint that determines complex biological, social and physical order.

The morphic fields suggested by biologists, embryologists and socio-biologists seem to have the most powerful effect between living creatures who have had a degree of direct contact. The energy field created through the contact appears to continue having an effect and influence on the animals and plants even after they are separated. For example, many animals have been shown to behave in an unusual fashion when another animal they have connected with is in some trauma, even when far apart and with no apparent means of communication. There are many similar situations where people have experienced an inter-connectedness that transcends time and space, too. Even when separated over great distances, and with no absolute knowledge of the event, people have often been affected in some way when those they love have an accident or die. I have twin sisters, and when they were young one of them would often know immediately if the other was in trouble, even when far apart. The way in which scientists explain such events is that an energy field is created by the meeting, by their relationship, and this has the power to influence them in a different way from 'normal' physical events in space and time. A relationship it seems is for life, not only for the time of meeting.

Physicists say that the only way to explain phenomena observed at sub-atomic level is that all particles remain connected with every other particle they have ever been in contact with. Physicists describe us as living in a hyper-connected universe.

They suggest it is this very trans-local connection, this web of interconnection, that makes up existence, not, as previously imagined, any particular particle, groups of particles, electrical charge or vibration. It seems it is relationships that create existence itself. Maybe love is not only all we need – love is all we are.

When a production team were filming a documentary about mental health care in rural China, the institutions they visited were barren desolate places, and the people in them were living empty despairing lives devoid of hope. They found only one man who smiled and seemed happy. He lived with the pigs, and whenever he was taken back into the house would simply leave and return to the pigsty. Eventually, he was allowed to make his home there. When asked why he alone seemed to be content he replied: 'I love the pigs and the pigs love me'.

When we make love we create an energy field, which exerts a powerful influence on the relationship

Love is the third force in every relationship. This force directly affects those in its energy field. Love is far more than just a feeling or emotion, and between sexual partners this body of love is so powerful that it can not only affect the lives of the two, but can also create new life. Two become one then three, the mystical equation of the alchemists, the holy trinity of relationship, the primal magic from which all else springs. On the physical level this love-energy creates future human beings; on the emotional level it creates a feeling of wellbeing, fulfillment and happiness; and on the spiritual level it becomes a source of healing, creativity, empowerment and wisdom. The love created by a couple in turn creates what they need for their love to continue. We love the love and the love loves us.

Conflict is necessary, as without it we could not make love

The field of love we create with our partners is not the same as the love we have for our partners and what they have for us. It is greater than the sum of the parts. For example, our partners cannot give us the unconditional love we may long for because they have also to think of themselves, and what they want will inevitably sometimes oppose what we want. If there is no such conflict an even deeper imbalance is happening that will reveal itself eventually, when the denied self-assertion explodes in some way.

When there has been emotional and physical intimacy over time and a strong body of love created, this does not mean there are no difficulties or struggles between you. On the contrary, the deeper the intimacy and love, the deeper the level of conflict that can emerge because it is safe to do so. The journey of love takes every couple into cultural and collective conflicts as well as personal and familiar ones. Like climbing a mountain, every plateau is followed by further even steeper and rugged terrain. The overarching designs of love, however, will ensure that a conflict surfaces only when the love made by the couple is strong enough to be able to digest it. Whether they decide to creatively engage the conflict or not is, of course, another matter.

Two women were in love, one from a working-class family, the other from a middle-class and wealthier family. In the beginning they enjoyed the differences, which were sources of interest and pleasure. Over time, however, subtle differences in language, expectation, lifestyle, and so on, lost their novelty and became a source of irritation and misunderstanding. There were fights as they felt judged by each other, or ashamed or rejected or hurt by the same differences that had once been so attractive.

Confronting each other was not helping, as it further emphasised their apparently irreconcilable differences. Eventually they turned away from attacking each other and linked in with their love. They sat side by side looking together at their difficulties. From this standpoint they could see that both had hidden vulnerabilities involved in these struggles, and that some of their fights came from a collective dimension, the personal fault of neither. For example, one knew the suffering that arose from being short of money, short of food, and worrying about how to pay the rent and bills. She would see the other's impulsive or frivolous purchases as irresponsible. The other, never having known financial insecurity, judged her partner as mean and over-anxious. Discovering the source of these different positions led to a deeper understanding of each other. They realised neither had been doing anything wrong. This made them both feel safer and they began to heal some of the hurt done through the class system in this country.

They continued their exploration and their love began to reveal to them deeper aspects of this cultural divide and the harm it had done. The woman from the working-class background cried over her buried shame that teachers had thought her stupid as a child because of the way she spoke, and how her whole family had felt inferior. Her partner was shocked, and while learning about the psycho-politics of our society received her partner's pain and held it in her love.

Later, another level surfaced – the working-class woman's rage at the collective betrayal of a whole class of people. This fury was turned on her partner who, with her unconscious assumptions of superiority, seemed to embody all that had hurt her. The partner began to look like an enemy. These women had created between them a body of love powerful enough to contain this intensity of feeling. They persisted with sharing everything they felt with the body of their love, trying to be as honest as possible, never denying their rage, blame or judgments, even when it felt wrong to feel superior, envious, suspicious and hostile. Although it was a turbulent ride, and there were times they felt so profoundly incompatible that they thought they would have to separate, they came through in the end. Their love grew and created a bridge between one of the most terrible divides in our culture. And in doing so they contributed to the healing of us all.

Love opens our hearts, not only to our partners, but to all life

Some of these collective woundings go very deep indeed, right into the heart of our human darkness. The greater the love-body we create, the more deeply we are confronted by the anguish of life, just as we also meet the joy. Love does not take us into a life full of happiness and no pain. For that we would have to be on another planet, if not another universe. The love between lesbians, for example, has the power to heal some of the terrible wounds between mothers and daughters, sisters, and between women everywhere, consequences of a patriarchy that divides women in order to rule over them. Even the divide between human beings and the rest of the animal world can be addressed in the intimacy of sexual love, since the beauty of the beast is in us, too. Our bodies are animals, and the way we relate to each other as animals is an integral part of intimacy, especially the instinctual bonding of sexual love.

Many are drawn to active politics to ease injustices and the suffering of people and animals; others redeem these collective pains within the inner domain of their intimate relationships. There are many examples of such cultural divides that can be healed and released within intimate sexual love – black and white, rich and poor, differences of class, caste, nationality and religion, parents and non-parents (in step-families, for example), and, of course, women and men. Each loving relationship can be a homeopathic remedy for the planet.

Similarly, on the more personal level, the more love you make, the deeper the conflicts that can and do emerge. But again only to the degree your love can contain and handle them. Bringing to the surface collective rage at class betrayal or deep introjected shame when you have only known each other for a few weeks would probably blow the relationship apart. Not enough love has been made yet to be able to hold such passion and anger and hurt, and so there would be no point, unless the person is motivated by some other agenda than creating loving intimacy, such as politics.

In most intimate sexual relationships, the more personal conflicts emerge before the bigger cultural divides reveal themselves. Otherwise, we could use the collective aspects of any conflict to either avoid its more personal dimensions, to attack our partners when we are hurt, or hide our vulnerability behind the political arguments. For example, a woman might attack her partner for being a dominating and controlling patriarchal male as a way to dominate and control him.

Love protects the relationship, as well as challenging it

Love brings into the relationship only what can be handled, and provides what is needed even when the individuals themselves do not know what to do. Almost all couples, for example, have some trouble adapting to the life of a new baby. However much joy and fulfillment there might be, there is usually some struggle and conflict when a couple first become co-parents as well as lovers.

A couple lived together for four years very happily before having a child together. The baby had difficulties feeding and cried a great deal. The couple found themselves so exhausted they could not even be bothered to argue. This happened despite each feeling irritated and hurt by the other's apparent neglect of their emotional needs while both were needing more than ever before. There was a spiral of resentment and misunderstanding that increasingly alienated them from each other. This meant they then got even less of what they needed. The mother became ill with appendicitis and was hospitalised for four days. During that time the father stopped work and cared for the three-month-old breast-fed baby using a bottle.

He continued to give the baby a bottle periodically even after his partner returned home. This lessened the demands on her while allowing him to develop a deeper bond with the baby. The mother was able to relax more than before and began to feel she had not completely disappeared into being a mother. The man, in caring physically for the baby, felt less helpless and proud to express his love in actions rather than feeling useless. He was also able to do things for the woman as she was still weak from the operation and clearly needed him, where previously she had been so involved in caring for the baby that she had seemed not to need him anymore for herself. The balance returned overnight.

This couple was too overwhelmed to find time for couples counselling, and too exhausted to talk in depth with each other, and so for this particular family, at this particular time, this crisis brought out exactly what was needed. Finding out why becoming parents had been so difficult for them, and examining the personal and cultural dimensions of parenthood, can take place later, if they want it to, when they have more time and are less exhausted. Telling the man that he should grow up and put his needs aside and support the new mother and baby for this period will not work. If he could have done this he would have done so already. Neither will telling the woman that she should not expect so much from her partner as he is a man and does not understand these things. Telling them both just to relax will only put more pressure on them. When you are exhausted, any input, however well-meaning, can be too much. Love came up with a solution that worked well for this particular family. For another family something completely different will need to happen. An unexpected windfall will mean help can be hired. A promotion at work and a house move will mean both partners will naturally re-engage in planning and creating a new life together. A friend who has gone through a similar process will offer helpful advice. The child may have special needs, which elicits more love from the parents, drawing them closer together. (Having a child with special needs is no tragedy, while having a child with no love to hold her is.)

Again and again I have observed situations where a force greater than the two individuals involved has created exactly the conditions needed for the love to flourish and grow. But if you do not look for these patterns, you cannot see them and what happens looks like random chance. Once you become aware of the patterns and balances of a relationship, it becomes natural to see them as the workings of a higher power – love.

Love always reveals the deeper meaning of behaviour

Love can work miracles in our daily lives, but it cannot force us to love, and whether we use these situations to create more love or not is completely up to us. What gets in our way, more than anything else, is that we think something is wrong when our relationships are not how we want them to be. Then we work hard on ourselves and our partners to be different, when whatever is happening is not wrong at all. It is more rewarding and revealing, as well as more creative and nurturing, to look at events as having their source in the relationship, the love. For example:

A couple is falling deeper into debt. The man walks out and refuses to discuss the situation whenever the woman brings the subject up.

We could conclude that the man needs to learn how to talk about things, that perhaps counselling would help him, and that there is little the woman can do other than share how she feels rather than attacking him, and be ready to listen when he's ready to talk. Linking, by consciously honouring the third force of a loving relationship (love) and developing a connection and communication with it, would try to discover what the love is attempting to do – *through* the man's walking out, *through* the woman wanting to talk, and through their growing financial stress.

This would first involve exploring together what might be the hidden meaning of the man's refusal to talk. It may be that he has tried to talk before, but that the woman has not listened. Perhaps she even hurt him by judging him when he tried. Perhaps the woman will not share the financial responsibilities, and although they are too much for him to shoulder alone, he would rather walk away than attack her for refusing to share the burden. Perhaps he is walking away and abandoning her in this context because she abandons him in another – maybe she has rejected him sexually when he approaches her to make love. Maybe the man feels irrationally ashamed about his failure to make enough money and doesn't know what to do, while his approaches to her for help have been so oblique that they have not been recognised. Perhaps the woman is angry because the man has hurt her in the past and so is starting conversations in ways calculated to make him feel guilty and bad, as a form of balancing the power. And it is this he is walking away from, not the finances.

Perhaps their love is creating a crisis in the relationship – externally in the form of money, internally in this breakdown in communication. In any healing crisis, first the body has to surrender to the disease. Here, the two may have accumulated so much mutual hurt and resentment, yet have ignored or buried it for so long, that their love is in danger of dying, and a crisis is the only way love can create the conditions where they will engage with their relationship again.

Once a relationship has reached crisis point, the only way to uncover these deeper dynamics is to enlist the greater wisdom of the relationship. It needs both of you for this exploration since separately you each have only half the picture. Linking works because it taps into this greater knowing, using the awareness of each partner as well as tapping into the love.

Linking is a process that connects individuals, couples and groups with the transcendental interconnectedness of relationship, whether between an individual and their own love or wisdom, etc, in an intimate sexual relationship, or in a family or a group of people gathered together for some common purpose. Linking will always bring a perspective greater than the individuals involved, as the whole is greater than the sum of its parts. Another example:

A woman spent money freely, and without consulting her partner, on designer clothes, expensive art, and pieces for the house. They tried to create a budget together but she repeatedly blew it. She seemed unable to stop, even when they began to get into debt.

Conventional wisdom would suggest that the woman needs treatment for her addiction to shopping, which might consist of a formal program, the 12-Step Program, or psychotherapy to uncover the roots of this behaviour. During this process her partner should be supportive and extend a patient understanding towards her as she struggles to deal with this. Linking into the love of the relationship, however, would take a different view and look at the behaviour in terms of the current relationship. What imbalance between them is this shopping trying to address? What are the hidden dynamics in their love that is leading to this situation? What is the context within which this shopping has meaning?

The couple actively began seeking the hidden symmetries and balances and found many hidden currents in the deep waters of their relationship. The man had been spending his energy as freely and wantonly with others outside the relationship as freely and wantonly as she had been spending their money, taking for granted her nourishment and support that allowed him to do this with confidence. There was a balance here. Finding this equivalence meant the woman felt less guilty and the man less judgmental. Another level of exploration could then begin.

They continued with the process and it emerged that the woman had a deep hidden sense of worthlessness. She felt she was not being cared for in the relationship as the man's psychology was so different. He had a strong sense of himself and could not imagine that anyone could have such a fragmented and insecure sense of themselves. The woman was therefore struggling with this alone, trying to give herself substance through buying things. She was also buying clothes and art to surround herself with beautiful objects in order to reflect back to her her own beauty as her fragile sense of self could not do this directly.

There was another dynamic. The man had experienced a lot of suffering as a child. The woman understood how this had made it hard for him to be in relationship, yet she could feel he wanted to learn and be healed of his suspicion and anxiety. She was balancing giving so much to him in this first phase of their life together by giving herself beautiful things. Her love was working hard knowing that one day this man would love her deeply and completely in return. Her love had chosen this man sensing his profound capacity for love, almost *because* he had known the darkness of hate and malice as a child. His capacity to love himself had allowed him to survive extreme conditions as a child. It also meant he was self-centred and ruthlessly put himself first. This caused her much grief, yet it was exactly this capacity to love oneself that she so much needed for herself. Others might say she should leave such a difficult man, but her love knew better. Very often what causes us the most trouble with our partners is the other face of something we long for. She needed the deep love he would eventually give her, so that the coldness she felt in her own heart towards her self would be healed. This is what happened.

In the next phase of their life together she was held in the warmth of his love in such a committed and determined fashion that she began to feel it was safe to be herself for the first time in her life. In love's synchronicity, she naturally stopped spending their money impulsively on things for the home at the same time that he stopped spending his energy impulsively outside the home.

Later still in their lives together, another dynamic revealed itself. Her 10-year shopping spree had burned through many of her consumerist desires so that she was free to follow what they both longed for – a simple life, close to nature. He had been less caught in the consumerist dream, having come from a wealthy background and seen that material possessions were not the route to happiness. She, having come from a poor family, had had to learn this through experience, which she did.

Their love healed in each of them devastating inner wounds that had nearly driven him to suicide and her to madness. They discovered together the context within which so much happening in the relationship had meaning. And this context was their love for each other.

Love is the context within which all behaviour in intimate relationships finds its meaning. When we have found the context within which a particular behaviour can be understood as having its source in some form of love, even when there may be many other factors operating, we are closer to the truth than any other process or explanation can take us.

CHAPTER SEVEN

Intimacy and Freedom

You were alone, I got you to sing.
You were quiet, I made you tell long stories.
No one knew who you were,
but they do now.
RUMI

Love and work require opposite skills

Some of what we do nurtures and supports love, while other things we do interfere and undermine love. The difficulty is that we often get the two confused. This is mainly because the skills that give us power and control in the world are often very different from those that nurture love in our lives. For example:

- We have developed various protections to prevent others from hurting us, such as keeping people at a distance, being false and putting armour on. Love, on the other hand, requires us to be open, available, unprotected and vulnerable.
- We have learned to experience ourselves primarily as separate individuals, yet love needs us to think about 'we' as much as about 'I'.
- When there's trouble, we have learned to take action, to *do* something. Love often needs us to experience what is happening without necessarily doing anything.
- We have learned to be polite and careful with what we say, so that we neither offend nor hurt people. Love asks us to be spontaneous and real without withholding or censoring ourselves, being honest even when we know our partners may feel hurt.

Here we can see how some of the skills we need to survive, to work, to make money and to build a life can interfere and undermine intimacy with our partners.

Intimacy holds both the heaven and the hell of human relationships

We both long for intimacy and are afraid of it. There are several dimensions to this. Firstly, intimacy with another is a journey into the unknown. However much we know about our partners, they remain essentially a mystery. True intimacy is the gift of oneself to another, and when two people are honestly intimate, this is a continuous source of wonder, never boring. What bores us is the predictable, the known, the lifelessness of repetition and deceit. Yet our fears of the unknown, of revealing ourselves, can make us hide from our partners, which leads to a painful emptiness in the heart of the relationship. The contrast of this with the delights of our earlier intimacy makes this lack of closeness even more painful, though we often do not realise our fear of being honest is what creates this.

Secondly, being intimate means that for a period we no longer experience the existential insecurity that comes from being a separate individual who alone is responsible for our life. Deep intimacy eases this existential aloneness. When making love, when sharing our deepest thoughts and feelings with our partners, we are no longer alone. The boundaries between us are blurred and we feel supported from being so close to another. Through this merging we are spared the pains of our separate existence and come to understand each other. To feel understood by our partners is a profoundly nourishing experience, just as not feeling understood is one of the most painful.

Thirdly, intimacy with those we love, especially in sexual love, takes us back to a lost paradise, to the natural spontaneity and blissful ignorance of childhood, before we learned we're separate and divided from each other and that we must curb our natural spontaneity. Leaving the innocent instinctual bliss of early childhood to enter the human community, with its self-awareness and existential aloneness, broke our hearts. In sexual intimacy, however, we enjoy again our natural spontaneity and freedom. All other relationships require us to contain aspects of ourselves. We can certainly be more free to be ourselves at home with our families than at the office, even more when partying with friends, but nowhere can we have the *complete* freedom that emotional and physical intimacy with our sexual partners allows us. We long for the innocence and freedom of true intimacy and find it intrinsically pleasurable. Yet it also challenges us. Intimacy rests upon us being transparently honest and sharing even aspects of ourselves we are ashamed or afraid of, or would prefer to keep hidden. The demands of intimacy are as great as the rewards.

Fourthly, the intimacy and closeness of sexual love includes the body, which brings us pleasures no other human activity can. Sexual love and the body are so important for intimate relationships that Chapters 12 and 13 explore the sexuality of love in depth. The pleasures of physical and emotional intimacy are reflected in the suffering we experience when we lose that closeness. Most of us have tasted the anguish of being with the one we love and yet feeling separate, estranged, distant, alienated or, for whatever reason, not able to be close to each other. Nelson Mandela said that he had never felt as lonely, not even in his years of solitary confinement, as when he was free and did not feel close to his wife. Intimacy, it seems, holds both the heaven and the hell of human relationships.

Four routes to intimacy

1. Letting down our defences

To be intimate with another involves putting aside our protective barriers, yet we have learned that if we do not protect ourselves we will be hurt. This is often the case, as life is a jungle as much as it is a garden. Not only that, but our protective defences are so automatic that they are part of our personality, which makes it hard for us to know when we are defending ourselves and building barriers to intimacy. We will go into this in more detail in Chapter 9.

2. Expanding our sense of self to include our partner

In our culture we identify with being a particular unique individual far more than we think of ourselves as part of a relationship. What we actually need, however, is to learn how to experience ourselves both as an 'I' and as part of a 'we'. This becomes possible only when we expand our sense of self to include those we love.

Learning to say 'I am me' is difficult for a young child. We begin by feeling ourselves as part of everything – even our parents are not seen as something separate from us. Eventually we realise we have our own identity and private inner world – that we are individuals. But when asked to commit ourselves to the 'we' of relationships as much as the T of the self, it is rather like being invited back into the ocean out of which we have so painstakingly crawled. Some of us solve this dilemma by remaining separate, others by submerging themselves and becoming lost in the relationship. True intimacy requires us to stay connected with both our individuality and our belonging to something greater than us – the relationship.

2. Putting aside our many 'doing skills and simply being'

Being intimate with our partners requires us to learn the art of being. Again, this is very different from the art of doing things we have mostly learned. In essence, this is what meditation is all about – learning the art of non-doing; in other words, experiencing life without always being driven to *do* something. Those who have tried meditation know this is hard enough alone, but when another is included it is more than twice as difficult, not least because of the intensity of feeling in intimate relationships. When we feel angry or afraid or insecure, it is much harder to just sit and feel this, yet intimacy often requires us to wait, do nothing and feel what is happening before acting to sort things out. Once again, the skills we have learned that are essential for our survival and success are not what nurtures love.

3. Letting go our self-control and being spontaneous

Loving relationships need us to be absolutely honest and transparent, yet revealing ourselves is the opposite of how we have been taught to behave. As children we were told to keep still and be quiet, not to let our bodies move spontaneously, and to stop shouting, kicking, spitting, pulling faces and jumping around. We were taught to say 'Please' and 'Thank-you', not to grab for things and run, that it was rude to say what we really thought, and that we must smile and be polite – all essential skills, else no nursery would have had us. As adults, too, keeping personal aspects private rather than naively revealing, being appropriate rather than spontaneous, and guarded rather than trusting, are all important. But what helps us survive in the boardroom does not necessarily help us in the bedroom. The spontaneous movements of our bodies in sexual intimacy and the transparency and honesty of emotional intimacy are radically different from our guarded privacy and self-control.

Being free to love and loving freedom are both essential for relationships

However much we long for the pleasures of intimacy, a major difficulty repeatedly surfaces throughout the life of a relationship – the conflict between the need for freedom and the need for intimacy. Although we all need both, most of us are usually more aware of our need for one rather than the other. And since opposites attract, we usually find ourselves drawn to a partner who manifests the opposite pole. This leads to many misunderstandings and arguments, with one partner demanding more closeness, more sharing and more self-revelation, while the other is demanding more space, less interference and more respect for difference. But this is where we get a good education from our lovers. We all need both intimacy and freedom, even when we may not know we do. Without freedom we have no integrity, power and authority, while without intimacy we have no connectedness, no closeness and no real meeting. In this conflict, as in so many others, it is very difficult for partners to teach each other for several reasons:

- Our partners are not distant authorities that we imagine are superior to us. We've seen them on Monday morning with a hangover.
- We are far more interested in teaching our partners to be nicer to us than learning from them about ourselves, such as how we behave on Monday mornings with a hangover.

- Our emotional involvement with our lovers can make us unreasonable, irrational and unpredictable. Just as they can be. Thank goodness. But this doesn't make for easy learning.

So what can we do? Firstly, understand how love works, then learn from love what needs to be done, if anything.

Understanding how love works and why intimate partnerships are so difficult makes us less likely to judge and condemn either ourselves or our partners when things are difficult. Knowing that there will inevitably be times when it seems impossible to resolve things, knowing that everyone has the same difficulties in different forms, however rich or famous or intelligent or beautiful, takes a pressure off. It also helps us realise that we are not the only ones living lives so different from the media images of sexual love – we are not so crazy or inadequate after all. Making sense of the chaos of our love life reduces our anxiety, and that always helps.

And when we turn to a force greater than our own will, such as our love, we tap into an energy that can guide and nourish us in a way nothing else can. Our love knows us and our own unique situation. It has a perspective greater than either individual. And it will never attack or undermine the relationship. This is important as there are many forces that operate against love. Apart from general fear and ignorance, there are many ways loving relationships can be undermined. For a start, there are a lot of false ideas about how loving relationships should be, which make us doubt and question our own. Also, most counselling and psychotherapy focuses on developing individual power and self-worth, finding what you need within yourself. While helpful in some ways, this ignores the equally important surrender of the self in the vulnerability of love. Another factor is that some people, unhappy in their own love life, find it painful to be around those who are. Their natural jealousy, especially if they do not acknowledge it, can undermine the love of others. Plus, there are the stresses and strains of modern living which, although materially comfortable in many ways, is hard – cut off from nature, surrounded by noise and traffic, with very little freedom at work and monthly bills to be paid else we might lose our home. All these create a climate that is not particularly supportive of love. Our love, however, will always be working for us, never against us. It will never harm us or the relationship, and will always work to create the best possible outcome for both, even if this involves separating for a while.

True intimacy rests upon the freedom to be apart. Loving relationships need both partners to have separate lives, as well as a life together; otherwise, coming together in intimacy has no depth. True intimacy is the gift of yourself to another. If there is no difference or separation, if we cannot be alone, then this gift is an empty offering. Love sometimes requires us to spend time alone, not in relationship, learning the value of freedom. Being alone and discovering freedom is an essential part of the journey into love. Though it may not appear love is at work when we are alone, it is, but in this book I am concentrating on how loving relationships work and so the focus is on relationship.

Being intimate creates Love

We make love through loving. It might be that we fall in love with the work of a particular painter. We find out all we can about them. We travel the world to see for ourselves their paintings. We examine their work in detail. We read about their life. We try to understand them, put ourselves in their shoes. If we can afford it we buy their paintings and hang them where we can see them as often as possible. In other words, we get as close as we can to the painter and their work. In this intimacy, our love brings us more insights into their genius, a deeper appreciation of their work and greater love for them than can any scientific or objective analysis. Much more revealing and challenging is falling in love with a person who also loves us.

It might be said that you can never know anything or anyone until you have been intimate with them. Many scientists, for example, say that we create what we see through our looking. Quantum and astro-physicists, looking at life from opposite poles of existence, are beginning to think of matter and the universe as being made of relationships and vibration, and that reality itself is a field of energy, not a set of objects. If this is the case, then it is not such a big step to say matter itself is made of love, that love is what matters, and that in the intimacy of our investigations we are making it. The human capacity to make love can manifest itself in any sphere of activity, including our genuine attempts to understand the mysteries of life. In the end we may find it is our very search, the same love of life, that is leading us to examine it so closely and try to understand it. And this is being reflected back to us in what we find. Maybe our curiosity did not kill the cat – maybe it created the cat. Or rather, the field of love between ourselves and the cat mutually created an is-ness called 'the cat and I'. Perhaps Schroedinger's cat lives in our heart and we only thought it could live in a box.

What is close and intimate is also cosmic and extraordinary

When we love each other we are engaged in a more sacred and mysterious act than we might realise. It places us at the creative source of existence. An ancient Tantric tradition teaches that we humans are responsible for making love for the whole universe, the love that even gods and demons need to go about their business. Other species and life forms may have different jobs to do, but divided as we are from both ourselves and each other, when we come together we make the love that makes the universe go round. We may think that what happens in sexual intimacy is a private affair, but like a stone thrown into a lake, the ripples spread over a wide area, perhaps through the whole energy field of existence. What is most intimate may prove to be the most powerful.

We all love someone or something and in doing so contribute to the love of us all. Even if we do not follow the path of love in intimate sexual relationships, we cannot escape love. Whatever path we follow in life will be determined by how our love is channelled – knowledge, art, fame, power, wealth, status, healing . . . Love has been defined as the capacity and willingness to suffer. To be alive at all, and willing therefore to suffer the often painful realities of life in a physical body, is itself an act of love. A pillow held over your face will soon show you, through the intensity of your fight to stay alive, how much you love life.

If we did not love life we would not be here, yet often this love lives only in our bodies, not in our minds. Consciously we are often preoccupied with planning our futures, working and struggling to get what we need and want, dealing with life rather than contemplating it. Yet whatever we spend our time doing and thinking, the reality hidden in all our hearts, in the dark interior of our bodies, is that we love life.

The love between us all, imperfect, turbulent and muddled as it is, collectively creates a vast energy field of love that extends around the planet. This great body of love in turn creates the conditions for love to grow among us. You might call this body of love God, Allah, fate, the higher power of the universe, the Tao, the quantum energy field that underpins existence, or any one of a number of names. But whatever name we give to the transcendental interconnectedness of us all, including animals and all life forms, we play our part in both its creation and its continued existence, whatever the form of love we contribute. We can deny, betray, undermine, attack or walk away from love, but we can never destroy it. What we are responsible for is simply whether we make it or not.

So how do we make this love that is so intimate yet powerful, so human yet so all-encompassing? In loving relationships there are five essential processes through which we create an energy field of love and begin to embody love. Each one makes love, brings love into life. These are:

1   Presence
2   Emotional closeness
3   Honest dialogue
4   Dealing with everything
5   Sexuality

We need all five. If any one of these is missing, our relationships become less loving. Let us look at each of these in turn.

CHAPTER EIGHT

The Art of Being Yourself

Let the lover be disgraceful, crazy,
absentminded. Someone sober
will worry about events going badly.
Let the lover be.
RUMI

It may seem obvious to say that we need to be ourselves and be present with our partners, but this is not as simple as it sounds. There is more to us than meets the eye. And there is a lot more to being with our partners than just sitting there. Being with our partners involves three processes, each one of which has levels and complexities beyond the simple fact of our being in the same room:

1 Bringing all aspects of ourselves to the relationship.
2 Embodying our energy, not only talking about it.
3 Simply *being* without necessarily *doing* anything.

These are inter-linked, but also have specific aspects.

1. We are far more than we think we are

We have within us a universe of possibilities and, like an iceberg, the greater part of us lies hidden. Some parts of us will never see the light and are not meant to – after all, our hearts are of darkness, and if they come to light, we die. Some aspects have been buried when we found they led to trouble, some aspects we have nurtured and developed. Each one of us has a unique combination of possibilities we have allowed and denied ourselves. But the denied aspects of our energy, though buried and forgotten, do not cease to exist. Whatever we might think, *all* of us are in the relationship. We might imagine we are always caring and sensitive and be unaware we have a ruthless and selfish side, or we may think we are organised and not realise we are chaotic in other areas. Our partners, however, experience all our aspects. In some ways we remain forever mysteries to each other, and in other ways our partners know us better than we do.

Living deep in our bodies and below our conscious minds are also the human possibilities denied by our present culture – for example, our kinship with other animals, the parts of us affected by the power of place, and the selves in contact with nature spirits, that can hear mountains and trees speak. Other cultures may have allowed these but disallowed other aspects, yet they all have their part to play in human consciousness and therefore our intimate relationships.

One way love helps us discover aspects of ourselves that we are not aware of is through the arguments we have with our partners. Arguments happen simply because we are different from each other, standing on different spots, viewing things from different perspectives. And our partners *are* different from us – we have chosen them for this very reason. Narcissus, in love with himself, was trapped in a hell. Only someone different from us can save us from ourselves, and only through loving what is different does our love grow.

For example, one person may be very willing to accommodate the other in choices about what to do and where to go, perhaps excessively so. The other may be more determined not to let what they want be pushed aside, and will always negotiate hard to get what they want. Both imagine that the way in which they do things is the right or best way. Since they do not question these habits, they also assume that this is what the other is doing. Over time a natural resentment builds up in the first one, which eventually explodes in an angry outburst at the other, who is amazed, having had no idea of the self-sacrifice that had been going on, especially as they would *never* do this. If the couple just attack each other – 'you are selfish, insensitive, uncaring', or 'you are needy, demanding, pathetic' – this could escalate. If, on the other hand, they stop looking at each other and instead look at the relationship, things become easier immediately.

1 They realise this problem affects them both and is one they would both like to resolve. They are on the same side and agree about this at least.

2 They realise they are up against one of those struggles that has its roots in the fact they are so different. If they know about love's hidden balance, they will know that this difference is the other face of something they need and love in each other.

3 Through being reminded of the positive side of this difference they become more willing to listen to each other rather than just reacting defensively.

4 By sharing how they feel – the anger of one and the defensiveness of the other – with the third force of love, they are not directly in each other's firing line and can therefore hear what is being said rather than just trying to fire or dodge the bullets.

5 This makes the situation safe and the underlying hurt in the one who has given

too much can surface, and the one who has done their own thing finds it easier not to feel guilty.

6 Both can realise that each has some of what the other needs. One needs to learn how to think of themselves more, the other to think of the other more. They have found the right relationship to teach them.

The pain of alienation from the one we love, forces us to deepen our understanding of love

When close to what is different from us we experience something radically different from being alone, and our love is forced to expand beyond itself. In this way we make more love. All relationships, of whatever kind, have degrees of similarity and difference. It takes sameness for there to be a meeting at all, though it is the differences that make the meeting interesting. We are attracted, like opposite poles of a magnet, to those who manifest different energies from the ones we are familiar with in ourselves. This is one way we encounter, through the relationship, dormant or buried aspects of ourselves. Love knows what it's doing, attracting us to our opposites.

In intimacy with someone different from us, we become connected with possibilities we lack. This leads to a wonderful feeling of wholeness and completeness, expansion and potential. However, all the delicious positive bonding of the honeymoon will eventually reveal its other face, its more negative aspects, as do all experiences on this bi-polar planet. It is only when the wonderful relaxation of feeling secure, loved and at peace becomes anger, alienation and misunderstanding, that we are challenged to create new ways of being and relating. Otherwise, we would all take love for granted. Perhaps gardening, cooking or keeping hamsters would then become the inspiration and source of literature, music and poetry. But I don't think so. That human love is so difficult and challenging is exactly what makes it so creative and compelling.

Love will always take us away from what is false and into what is real

Our partners, more than anyone else, confront us with aspects of ourselves we would probably prefer not to know about. For example, we may imagine we are sensitive to others but in fact can use our alleged sensitivity to bully others, or we may think we are easy-going whereas in reality we are only that way when we get what we want. Our partners relate with who we really are, not our beliefs or stories about ourselves. Even if they have initially believed us, that we are relentlessly wonderful, and even if we believe this ourselves, the person our partner actually lives with is the real person. And most of us would prefer to live with a real person than a perfect one. And, of course, it works the other way around – if we mistakenly think we are a worthless failure, our partners know differently and will slowly teach us this, too. Love will always show us what is false and help us be real.

With our love present as a midwife, giving birth to new parts of ourselves is much easier as love welcomes parts of us into the relationship even when our partners, out of fear, do not. Just as the same love will unconditionally accept our partners even when we cannot. The release of buried energies within one partner will lead to a corresponding release in the other, each helping the other give birth to themselves.

A couple met, fell in love, married and had a wonderful honeymoon. They felt they were soul mates and destined to be together. The trouble began when the woman had a new manager at the office where she worked. The changes being introduced left her with far less freedom and this made her unhappy. To begin with, her partner took care of her and she would forget work and enjoy their nights out together and feel better when they cuddled in front of the TV. Gradually, the unhappiness ceased to change even when the man bought her flowers, offered to take her out for a treat or held her in his arms. He began to feel irritated and short-tempered with the way she was handling her difficulties, and suggested she be more assertive or just did what she wanted anyway. But the woman was not able to challenge the manager or 'have it out with him' in the way her husband told her to.

One day the man lost his temper and for the first time in their relationship spoke to her sharply. He told her how he was fed-up with listening to her moans, that she was weak and pathetic and he was going out with his mates to escape. He came back drunk. She was weeping, which enraged him further, and he shouted at her. She was shocked, as he had never raised his voice to her before. In fact, it had been his gentleness that had first attracted her, as he was so unlike her father, who had a violent temper. Her father had, in fact, so frightened her as a child that she had lost her natural assertiveness, which is why she was having trouble at work.

For a moment she was torn between running away to her mother's to escape, and turning around to face and engage with her husband. Fortunately, she faced him. For the first time in her life she began to feel angry and express it. Once she had begun, a lifetime's rage and fury began to pour out. It was his turn to be shocked. He was torn between wanting to hit her to shut her up, and sitting down to find out what all this was about. Fortunately, he sat down. Even though he could grasp hardly anything of what she was saying, the fact he had sat down made all the difference to her. Her father would have hit her. She then burst into tears and fell into his arms. Again he had no idea what was going on but he held her, relieved that she was at least no longer attacking him. He stroked her hair and she gradually came to her senses. They talked.

The woman had told him many times previously how glad she was he was not like her father. He, knowing he could be violent and having had a violent father, too, had worked hard to control himself and be gentle with her, though when drunk some of his real feelings of frustration had emerged. Although parts of her had wanted to run away, she had responded. The very energies she had been trying to keep out of the relationship – his anger – had been exactly what she had needed to trigger her own buried aggression. This, in turn, would help her negotiate more effectively at work to get what she needed. Meanwhile, her willingness to fall into the tears and hurt underneath her anger helped the man connect with the tears and hurt lying in wait for him underneath his anger when the time came for that. Although the woman had thought she had chosen the man for his sensitivity and gentleness, she had more deeply chosen him for his capacity for anger and assertiveness.

It was their love that made her turn around to face him, and that made him sit down and listen. Their love led them to contradict all the impulses within them to do the opposite. Through their love they broke the patterns of generations before them and new dimensions to their relationship opened up. A great journey had begun that night.

2. We meet ourselves and our partners most intimately through the body

Dimensions of who we are beyond our personality come into play in sexual relationships more than others, as the energy of the body is involved. Thoughts and feelings we try to banish do not just disappear – they live on in our bodies. We do not, therefore, encounter our deeper selves by thinking or talking about them, but only by experiencing them. We embody energies when we *feel* them. It is not enough, for example, to say we are angry unless we also feel it. When we experience our anger in our guts, when we breathe deeply so we feel it all the more, we *embody* our anger and, as a consequence, become more present. The more we feel emotions in our body, the greater our capacity to feel generally, and this is essential for loving relationships and sexual love. It also works the other way around. When we stop ourselves feeling angry, sad, afraid, confused or whatever, we stop other feelings, too.

We cannot let be in others what we do not let be within ourselves, and when we do not feel our anger, fear, sadness, or other feelings and sensations, then we cut off from our partners to the same degree we are cutting off from ourselves. If, for example, we condemn and cut off from our own anger or fear, then we will similarly condemn our partner's anger or fear, telling them not to be so aggressive or to pull themselves together. We will not then listen to what their anger or fear is trying to communicate.

Whenever we reject unwelcome feelings, we lose some of our capacity to love and be loved. But love always works to bring to the surface whatever is blocking the flow of love. And intense feelings, however much we try to keep them out of the relationship, will in some form or other emerge in the prolonged contact of daily intimacy. We can control what happens and keep a relationship 'safe' when we keep our partner at a distance, but as soon as we begin to create a life together, things happen, especially things that make us angry, insecure, afraid, needy or whatever it is we have tried to avoid. Sexual love makes us feel a lot, and needs us to feel a lot – there's no way around this.

Letting our bodies move freely will release buried feelings

The most direct way to connect with lost feelings is to give our bodies freedom to express themselves. The feelings are held in the tensions in our muscles, in the restriction of our breathing, in the rigidity of our movements, and so on. Moving the body and breathing deeply brings these feelings to the surface again.

A Linking process that helps here involves the couple sitting side by side, facing an empty chair or some symbolic representation of the body of their love – the relationship.

Breathe deeply with your eyes closed. After five minutes let your body move and make sounds. To begin with you might feel uncomfortable, want to stop, laugh, or make fun of the process out of fear or embarrassment, but go through this point and let your body take over. If you want to shout but are worried about making too much noise, then shout into a pillow. You can jump around, shout or stamp. You can dance, drum, sit and sway. You can shake, cry, scream, or punch a cushion, strangle it, hold onto it or stroke it. Do whatever you feel. After 10 minutes of this, face each other and repeat: 'I love you and I'm afraid of you, I love you and I'm afraid of you, I love you and I'm afraid of you . . .' for as long as you have previously agreed. This might be 10 minutes or half an hour. Even if we do not feel this fear, saying this is powerful and revealing. It releases tensions between you that neither knew were there.

At the end of this phase, hold each other in silence for as long as you wish. Then you can put on some music and dance, go for a walk together, talk about what happened, plan a holiday, or do whatever feels right. You do not have to share anything about the experience if you would rather not, as it is the energetic process itself that is doing the work of unblocking the flow of love between you, not really what you say.

This exercise is worth repeating whenever you feel the energy is blocked between you, or that something is wrong but you don't know what. Each time you do it will be different, as you cannot step into the same river of energy twice. It is particularly helpful for those who do not use language as their primary medium of self-expression, but prefer action and doing things, using their body to express themselves. These people have a hard time with more traditional ways of handling difficulties in relationship, such as talking things through, counselling, reading books like this one, and so on.

When life flows freely through our body, so does love

Whenever a sensation or feeling hurts too much or is too threatening, then we tense our muscles in order not to feel it. Over time, this tension becomes a chronic contraction in our body that we no longer notice and which restricts the amount of life we can feel. This protects us from pain, but limits our capacity for love and pleasure. The Linking exercise described above helps bring our bodies back to life, and we literally incorporate the energies of life we have been missing or have lost. More life, and love, flows through our bodies and when our life force (our *chi*) flows freely. We become more physically present with our partners and there is a richness when we make love, which in turn brings even more parts of ourselves and our partner to life.

Sexual love resurrects the body from its numbness and immobility and we find ourselves feeling a whole array of emotions and sensations with our lovers that may at times feel strange. We may shake, weep, feel enraged or very anxious, irritated or rejected. We may feel deeply upset for some apparently trivial reason, worried that our partner may die, feel desolate and abandoned when they are 10 minutes late, find ourselves hating them more than we can remember hating anyone before because of some remark they make. These irrational feelings may be disturbing, but are really signs that our bodies are coming back to life. So, rather than running from them, we should welcome them, as signs that love is working through our bodies to enable us to make yet more love.

3. Love needs us to learn the art of being

The third aspect of being present with our partners lies in simply being with them, not only doing things with them. Young children and animals naturally let themselves be. They live in the here and now, not in the future or past. A baby will look at you in the naked simplicity of being, as do wild animals and birds – there is no barrier. We have learned to hide ourselves from such raw meetings and can find simply being with another without doing anything unbearable. Even when sitting silently with someone there are likely to be many things we are doing internally other than just being there. We may be worrying about work or wondering what the other is thinking, we may be trying to create a good impression or working out how to get what we want from the situation. To simply *be* with another is not as easy as it sounds, yet the most intimate meetings are when neither is doing anything other than simply being there.

To learn the art of being, here are some Linking Exercises.

1 Sit facing each other and retain eye contact for 10-20 minutes without saying anything. Set a clock so that you will not have to look away. Do this either holding hands or remaining separate. You may feel uncomfortable at times. There may be tension in your body, unaccustomed feelings can surface, you may find yourself hardly breathing or in physical discomfort. Stay with the exercise through these moments and you will find an ease on the other side. You have crossed over a threshold into a new way of being together.

2 Repeat the above exercise but with one for half the time doing the looking and the other being seen. Then switch over. Notice which you find easier – seeing or being seen. How does this relate with the way you behave with each other?

3 Again sit facing each other, having set a clock so that you are not distracted. For 10-30 minutes, holding hands or not as you wish, retain eye contact and say whatever comes to you. Any thought or feeling, any pictures or concerns of any kind. What you say does not have to make sense. Let the words come without them necessarily having any meaning you immediately understand. There may be times when you are silent or times when you are both speaking. What you say may be connected with what your partner has just said or may have no apparent connection whatsoever. Again, you will cross over a threshold, your familiar habitual reactions and responses giving way to unpredictable and spontaneous utterings that may not be anything like your normal speech. When we speak from our being and not our doing minds, a different quality of conversation evolves.

4 Practice being silent together, which is generally more difficult for one than the

other. Walk along a beach holding hands and saying nothing. Look at a view standing side by side without saying how beautiful it is, just receiving it. Sit together with a drink without the usual gossip. Simply sit side by side holding hands, imagining yourself surrounded by your love.

5 In a safe place, one of you closes your eyes or is blindfolded and the other leads them around. Change over. Do this when you are not in a fight as the one who cannot see is very vulnerable. Notice how you feel. Does leading or being led feel more familiar? Were you anxious, and if so in what way? For the one leading, notice how the other is reacting and reduce the speed of your progress until they are comfortable with what you are doing. Notice the involuntary reactions that teach you how to remain in tune with the other.

6 Walk through the streets holding hands, with only one talking, beginning every sentence with: 'Now I am aware of . . .' and completing it, reporting to the other in a continuous monologue everything that is in their awareness each moment. This may be a sight, a smell, a memory, a worry, a thought, a hope, a fear . . . anything at all. 'Now I am aware of a person coming towards me. Now I am aware of trying to move out of the way. Now I am aware of the sky. Now I am aware of wondering if it is going to rain. Now I am aware of worrying because I have not got an umbrella. Now I am aware of being irritated with you for not remembering to bring an umbrella . . .', and so on. Do this for half an hour to an hour and then change over. We tend to assume our partners are more like us than they are simply because we do not know how others experience life. This exercise gives you a glimpse into each other's internal world and can surprise you with how different you actually are.

7 Do some of the above exercises naked – which ones are entirely up to you!

Working side by side and facing each other are different ways of relating – love needs both

Love is created primarily in two ways. One way involves working alongside others with a common purpose. When we do something, create something, work towards a common goal in a team or partnership, we make a particular kind of love. The more we focus on the common goal, the less we are concerned for our personal situation, defending our position, keeping our image intact, fulfilling our private desires, and so on. When we commit ourselves to a common goal so completely that there are no separate egos involved, no hidden agendas or ulterior motives, something magical happens. A collective integrity evolves, a true community of individuals, and love is made. Some activities more easily lend themselves to this, such as climbing a mountain or struggling against political oppression. Yet in any area of human endeavour where we work alongside others for a common purpose, such as building a house, bringing up a child, organising a festival or cooking a meal, love can be made between everyone involved.

I lived in a community for many years where we were committed to creating a new way of being, building a community based on freedom, truth and love (it was the time for these things in the '70s!). In our different ways, we struggled to make our dream a reality. Even now, more than 20 years later, when I meet anyone from that time there is immediately love there, even when we may have nothing in common any longer and may not even like each other. Maybe we never liked each other, yet still there is love, whether we want it or not. Working side by side, connections happen and the love grows by itself.

The love made by working together is impersonal. A more personal love grows when we turn and face each other. This love involves us stripping down our defences and standing naked, transparent to the gaze of the other, daring to see and be seen in our entirety. Being present, doing nothing, simply being, makes us utterly vulnerable to the other. There is nothing to protect us, no defensive barrier. Whatever the other does will affect us as there is nothing in place to keep them out. When two people encounter each other in this vulnerable transparency of being, they are making a gift of themselves to the other, and love simply happens. In counselling and psychotherapy, the deepest healing is when neither client nor therapist is doing anything, when both are simply being together and there is no separation from each other and the truth. Both are witnessing and experiencing together the reality of our human predicament, and both are healed in that moment by a force greater than the two of them in their separate roles – love. There is always at those times a recognition of our helplessness and a surrender to the truth, a non-doing being together, which is very different from the way we normally relate.

Partnership and family involve both forms of love. We continually move between facing each other in intimacy and closeness, and standing side by side facing the world and working together to make a home and care for any children. In a loving relationship there are therefore many opportunities to create love. And when sex is involved the possibilities expand further. Sex is love in the body, and when love is present in the body, the sexuality of love naturally flows. And when we make love with our bodies, there is not only healing and pleasure, but the power to create life itself.

When completely present in the silence and stillness of non-doing being, we are utterly open to the moment. This is the source of wisdom. When gathered together with others, simply being present with each other, whatever is the truth and power of that community is revealed and can be experienced and witnessed. And when our body is simply present with our partner's body, in the natural spontaneity of sexual love, this is the reality through which new life and new love come into being. Being present is the oldest, most primitive and yet most potent and creative force in existence.

CHAPTER NINE

Protected on the Streets, Naked Between the Sheets

The way of love is not a subtle argument.
The door there is devastation.
Birds make great sky-circles of their freedom.
How do they learn it? The fall, and falling.
They're given wings.
RUMI

Without physical and emotional closeness we cannot make love. Yet what sounds simple, being close to those we love, is also difficult, as we both long for intimacy and are afraid of it. Whenever we are close to another with our protective defences down, we can be hurt, and even though it often appears that one is resisting closeness and the other is open to it, in different ways we are all afraid of deep intimacy.

Some protect themselves by trying to control the relationship, and others by not fully engaging in the relationship. The first will demand of their partners that they share more, express how they feel, engage more, while the second will demand of their partners that they leave them alone, that they stop demanding, and that they give them more space. This is familiar scenario to many of us in intimate sexual relationships, especially as we are attracted to those who embody the opposite polarity energetically to ourselves.

The relationship has the answers we seek

With conflicts of this nature, where the attraction and the fights are linked, we find the resolution not within the two individuals, but in the relationship, in the hidden reciprocity underlying what is happening. Here's how:

1 Realise that neither you nor your partner has the whole picture.
2 Realise, too, that each will have certain elements, insights or energies that are needed for deeper understanding to emerge.
3 Assume your partner, however wrong they seem, has a view that can teach you something new about them, the relationship, yourself or all three.
4 Put yourself in the other's shoes, see through their eyes and feel the world the

way they do. For example, have the same argument with each playing the role of the other. Put your body into a posture similar to theirs. Say some of the same phrases they do.

5 Whatever it is you are accusing your partner of, actively look for the hidden symmetry where you are doing exactly the same, though less obviously.

6 When you find it, let them know. You don't need to apologise, just tell them how it is.

The symmetry of the relationship reveals the deeper grammar of love

The magic lies in that whenever one or both partners sincerely look for the hidden symmetry, the relationship naturally re-aligns itself. Once you find the deeper grammar generating the conflict, where both are doing exactly the same thing in different ways, the resolution is already beginning. What's more, this does not necessarily have to be done together. If one person goes through this process, let's go their position and opens to love, then the other is synchronously moved in some way to let go and open up, too.

Our defences protect us, but they do not always serve us

We have learned to control what happens to us in order not to be harmed. This control is absolutely essential to develop the power to create or do anything – even amoebae control what aspects of their environment they will allow through their cell wall and what they keep out. In humans, this control is conscious and deliberate and, though essential for our survival, it is a major obstacle to intimacy.

We are first driven to develop power over life to avoid our extreme helplessness as a baby, and in the beginning our first power is over our bodies. Later, we notice that when we smile or cry it has an effect on others and we learn to use our self-control to have a degree of control over others, trying to make sure we get what we need. By the time we are adults, our protective strategies for controlling others have become automatic, and we no longer know when we are being open and when we are controlling things.

For example, one person may think it is natural to always look for someone's weak spot in order to have a degree of power over them. They assume that everyone does this and so it makes sense to be prepared since relationships are power battles. Their partner, as usual, inhabits the other pole, and believes that relationships are about nurturing and taking care of each other, or at least they should be. Naturally, they will fight about this difference, challenging each other's belief system and resisting each other. The resolution of the fights will each time bring them closer to realising that there is truth in what each is saying. This is important as many of our protective habits are self-fulfilling. If we approach others expecting a power battle and so come on heavy, a battle for power is what we're likely to find. If we run away from intimacy because we fear being abandoned and left alone, alone is how we will end up.

We have all turned away from a full relationship to protect ourselves

As children, we had to find ways to lessen the impact of reality as it was often too much for our young egos to cope with. When we eat we chew food and break it down into its component parts, we absorb the nutrients and eliminate the rest. We digest experience in the same way. When young we do not have the equipment to digest all the ideas, emotions, pressures and beliefs fed to us. We cannot break them down and discriminate between what is good for us and what is not. To cope, we find ways to avoid the full impact of the relationships that both sustain us and overwhelm us.

All living things have evolved ways in which they defend themselves against being killed or made a part of something else – anything without protection against being eaten would have become extinct long ago. The animal in us knows how to survive, and every technique an animal has evolved to ensure their survival – to fight, flee, hide, disguise, placate, seduce, puff up, play dead, undermine, poison, weave webs, camouflage, create alliances – has an equivalence in our human armoury. If you don't know the ways you protect yourself through controlling what happens in relationship, ask your partner – they'll know.

There are essentially five ways to protect oneself in a relationship.

- A flight from the relationship – by being unreal and hiding our true selves (like the person who always fits in to please others as a way to avoid being seen, much like a chameleon).
- A rejection of the relationship – either by:
  (i) Denying the need for a relationship and trying to go it alone (like the lone ranger who never reveals his weak side, and rides off into the sunset all alone),
  (ii) Refusing to grow up and take responsibility for the relationship (like the person who asks with a helpless air 'Can you do it for me?', much like a young bird with its mouth open).
- A fight with the relationship – either by:
  (i) Trying to control things overtly through bullying (like the person who walks around aggressively and always puts others down).
  (ii) Covertly through undermining the relationship (like the person who seduces you while looking all the time for any weakness that can later be exploited).

- A resignation in the relationship, which is loving and caring on the surface but underneath is angry and jealous (like the servant who is apparently supportive until their employer is vulnerable, at which point they enjoy a spiteful revenge).
- A distance from relationship – love is there but the other is kept at a distance (like the lover who does not declare his love because his ideas of morality forbid it).

These defence patterns are well-known to psychoanalysts and have been given names like schizoid, psychopath and masochist, but we can call them the chameleon, the lone ranger, the baby bird, the bully, the seducer, the servant and the stoic. Whatever we call them, though, these protective behaviours served us well when we were growing up, but in the intimacy of our adult love affairs, they get in the way. Ask your partner which ones they think are your favourites, and tell them theirs. Each one, of course, has its more positive side. The chameleon is very sensitive; the lone ranger very respectful of others' freedom; the young bird is appealing and caring; the bully is often very generous; the seducer is charismatic and sexy; the servant is loyal; and the stoic is honest and reliable. You can imagine how any combination of these could fall in love and, to begin with, enjoy each other greatly. Then later . . .

Most conflict in intimate relationships is a war of protection systems

Here is the difficulty. We develop our power to protect our vulnerability, but without being vulnerable we cannot be close to anyone. Our protections, so important on the streets, are interfering with what happens in between the sheets. So what do we do when we long for the intimate contact with our partners that makes love, while without realising it we are automatically protecting ourselves? How can we, for example, easily listen to our partners if we were told as a child that we were stupid and so stopped listening to what others said about us? Or, if we were punished when we got angry, and taught that to be angry is wrong, how can we be honest with our partners when we feel angry with them?

We cannot simply listen to what our partners say, as they may be telling us things about ourselves – as part of *their* defence system, and not because it is the truth. For example, they may say 'You are trying to control me!' as a way to try to control the other, or 'You're too defensive!' when naturally they are. This is a kind of attack. Through the conflicts and fights we have with our partners, the relationship gradually shows us how we defend ourselves without knowing what we are doing.

Most chronic conflict (the fights that happen time and time again) can be seen as a war of protections systems, a conflict between the strategies each has adopted to protect themselves from conflict, like the Mutually Assured Destruction program of the Cold War – MAD it was called. By resolving such conflicts we learn about our defence patterns as well as discovering the pleasures of relaxation and peace that come with disarmament. Linking in with our love helps because we can sense that our love does not judge or criticise us and so we have less need to be defensive. And though there are times when we cannot trust each other, we can always trust our love.

A lawyer protects herself from feeling hurt by intellectually analysing what is happening rather than feeling anything. This gives her great skill in explaining and understanding, which makes her a good lawyer, but which leaves her cut off from her emotions. Her partner, an actor, is very different. He protects himself by creating emotional dramas that distract himself and others from the real issues. He is therefore more intuitive and feeling, which makes him a good actor, but he has difficulty analysing and explaining himself. When things are going well, these different strengths and weaknesses complement each other. But when there's trouble . . .

The woman does not realise that her intellectualisation is a defence. She thinks the way to resolve arguments is to analyse, explain and logically explore the two positions. She is not aware that her partner cannot do this. The man is equally convinced that the way to proceed is to let the emotions out, express the feelings and feel what is going on. He is not aware that his emotional expression can easily overwhelm her, just as her legal arguments and logic can overwhelm him. Each is convinced they are right, which further entrenches them in their opposing positions.

Another couple has a different dynamic.

One man learned to protect himself from his parents' anger by escaping into a fantasy world. Another man avoids the powerlessness he knew as a child by trying to control everything. The first man feels powerless in the real world but has the capacity to simply be, the other has a capacity for doing much, but has little experience of simply being. They bring complementary gifts to the other. Until there's trouble. Then the escapist tendencies of the one will infuriate the practicality of the other. The force of his frustration then threatens the first, who retreats even further into his private world. Hurt and angry at this abandonment, his partner becomes even more frustrated and attacking, and the cycle continues.

If conflicts are not resolved but are just put aside or swept under the carpet, they spiral deeper into 'mutually assured destruction'. Eventually, the love in a relationship will precipitate a healing crisis where each is presented with a choice – which is more important, the relationship and the love, or the protection and control? This point is usually reached through some crisis. In the first example above, the emotional dramas might lead to an accident, or the intellectualisation to such an alienation from feeling that clinical depression sets in. In the second example, one may escape so far into fantasy that he loses touch with reality, or the other may become so enraged that he is violent. It is often a crisis that confronts us with the consequences of what we have been doing and gives us the chance to change things. By talking to the body of their love as if they were appealing to a third party they could both trust, in both these examples these couples could more easily begin to understand the true nature of their differences. Sitting side by side for a start immediately unlocks the head-to-head destructive cycle of recrimination and blame, and each can feel heard by the body of their love, even if not by each other.

We need to learn ways of protecting ourselves that respect love rather than undermine it

During a crisis or serious trouble we are more likely to reach out for help, go to counselling, seek advice from friends, tune in to the body of our love, meditate, talk more openly to each other, break patterns of relating that once seemed natural to us, and so on. And it is only when we realise that our protections no longer serve us that we explore better ways of protecting ourselves than avoiding the reality of relationship.

As children we could not articulate clearly how we felt, negotiate, walk away, assert our own authority, or engage in emotional dialogue in the same way we can as adults. All these strategies for dealing with difficulties were not possible when we were young as they require a maturity and power we did not have then. Mature protections do not diminish our capacity for love or limit relationships – they respect them. Neither does seeking help, going to counselling, meditation, Linking into love, being more honest, sharing more of ourselves, reflecting on the consequences of our actions, staying when our habit is to walk away, walking away when our habit is to stay, feeling fear when our habit is to feel angry, or feeling anger when our habit is to feel fear. In other words, it's necessary to let our love, rather than our fear, guide us. These strategies for dealing with difficulties all support love – they do not undermine it as do the protective habits we developed as children, when all we could do was diminish our involvement in a relationship.

Love brings to the surface our buried hurts so they can be healed

We learn more constructive and mature ways of protecting ourselves only through the challenge of relationships. As always, love has designed it so that we get exactly the partners we need to teach us what we most need to learn. In the symmetry of loving relationships, we are drawn to those who will wound us in ways similar to our first experiences of being hurt by others. This is partly because we are attracted to our opposites energetically, and this includes those with opposing defence mechanisms, and partly because to have our childhood needs met, we need someone who can reach into where we most need their love, which is the same spot where we have been hurt. So to get the love we long for, we have to risk being vulnerable where we are most afraid of being hurt.

> A man had grown up in a family with an absent father. He had loved his mother and she had used him as a substitute for a husband. This made her life less painful as he, unlike her real husband, was there and did his best to take care of her. But for the boy, this was a heavy pressure. He could not be her husband, however much he tried, as he was a child and not a man. As a man he was very attractive to women because he knew how to take care of a woman emotionally, how to be very close to her, but he would not commit himself to any one woman as the demands of such a relationship looked very dangerous to him. He did not want that pressure and responsibility again.
>
> Meanwhile, a woman had taken on, as a child, the role of mother in her large family. She was the eldest and her mother was often depressed and withdrawn, partly because of the lack of support from her husband who often disappeared for lengths of time. This woman worked hard as a child, taking on the role of both mother and father for her siblings. Through this she became very able to give others what they needed, but found it difficult to take care of herself.
>
> These two met and fell in love. The man gave the woman the intimacy that her lonely and hard-working childhood had deprived her, and she gave him the nurturing that taking care of his mother had deprived him. After a long honeymoon, the other side of things began to emerge. The woman needed the nourishing intimacy he gave her so

much that whenever he did not give it, she demanded it, almost as her right – just like his mother had done. Meanwhile, the man kept escaping from the responsibilities of being an adult and the inevitable demands and pressures of being in a relationship, and would disappear and abandon her-just like her parents had done. Each gave the other both what they had lacked and also what had hurt them.

There is usually deep disappointment that the original promise of the relationship, to save each from pain and loss, is not fulfilled. Or at least, that is how it appears to begin with. Love always keeps its deeper promise though – to make enough love to heal all the wounds in both. This is why old wounds from childhood are brought to the surface in intimate sexual love. The difficulty is that old hurts tend to emerge during fights and it feels exactly as if our partners are *causing* the pain, rather than merely triggering it.

When this happens, as it usually does, there is the potential for deep healing. But first the wounds have to come to light. In homeopathy, naturopathy, Ayurveda, Chinese medicine and other healing traditions that work to heal the whole body rather than just suppress the symptoms, cures usually involve the disease worsening for a period before the body begins to heal itself in a new way. It is the same for the body of love in a relationship.

The heartbreak caused by loving can only be healed by daring to love again

Though it may feel like a betrayal and a disappointment when we are hurt by our partners, it is actually the fulfillment of a promise love has made to us all, that when we turn to love we will be healed. Disappointment is often the trigger that brings to the surface some of the sense of betrayal that underlies the compromises we adopted as children in order not to be hurt. As children we naturally love our families, and equally naturally this will cause hurt along the way. Ancient Chinese wisdom has it that our hearts have to break seven times in order to fully open. The first break involves the realisation that our parents do not love us in the same complete way we love them (in another tradition this has been described as the Oedipal conflict). When we meet a partner and fall in love, we are opening up to the possibility that our love can be a joyous thing, not only something that will lead us into heartbreak again. Letting go our habitual protective behaviours is a vital part of this process.

Whether we choose to move into a new level of vulnerability with our partners or choose to remain protected, love is still operating. Our self-protection evolved simply because we felt ourselves worth defending. We are developing a love of ourselves to make our loving another, when the time comes, worthwhile, though the fruition of that love may be with a different partner. The same process is usually experienced in love whether with a sequence of partners or with the same partner in a sequence of experiences. Whether we make love with one partner or many, we all either repeat the same mistakes or make enough love to move through our fear into a deeper level of love.

When we are courageous enough to truly love someone, we are inviting into our lives a higher power than our protections and defences, and our love will be more than we bargained for – both more terrible and more wonderful. Love will demand that we work on every single thing that gets in the way of our capacity for love and take us deeper into love, each step designed to meet exactly what we need and to challenge us to the maximum we can handle. After all, love only has the time we are alive to teach us how to love. Every way we have developed of holding back from the truth and reality of our relationships will be challenged repeatedly by love in intimate sexual partnerships. True marriage is not the ceremony in the church but a commitment to go on this journey together, where there is nowhere to run to and nowhere to hide from love.

Once we commit ourselves to love, we eventually discover that what we have been defending against, protecting ourselves from all this time, is simply life, and that the great truth, mostly unconscious and known only by our bodies, is that we love life. We have been protecting ourselves from our own love. The secret hidden in all our hearts is that we love ourselves, we love others and we love all life, and that we always have and always will. It's better to discover this truth before we die, otherwise death will be an agony of remorse, not a release. The agony of death is not the death itself, but the realisation as we leave this life that we have never really loved it enough. As an old African saying advises: 'When Death comes to find you, let him find you alive. And even better, in love'. So, when you fall in love, keep falling.

of an exploration rather than the end to it. Often we don't know what is going on, and pressure from our partners to explain or speak can make things worse. Speaking of our confusion, anxiety and bewilderment to the relationship is easier than to a hurt and angry partner who is pressurising us. There are many ways in which using your relationship as the mediator can help communication. There are some Linking exercises at the end of this chapter that suggest practical ways to use your love in this way to help you understand each other.

The capacity to tell both truth and lies is essential

As often as communication builds bridges, it can divide us. One of the keys that makes the difference is whether we are being honest or not. But there are differences between being honest, telling the truth, and not lying. And none is as simple as might at first appear.

It is essential to be able to lie. Without the capacity to lie we can have no inner life. We would be transparently available to anyone who cared to look. Living in such utter vulnerability, with no privacy or inner safety, would destroy us. We would never be able to grow up and leave our parents, we would not be able to negotiate or do deals, and neither would we be able to enjoy dinner parties or relax in the company of others. We would not be able to gestate anything in the dark privacy of our own inner space, and as a result would have no creativity, no freedom and no self.

To be uniquely ourselves and claim the authority of our own experience, we must be practiced at the art of deception. When Adam and Eve hid from God, this was the real subversion of his authority and the beginning of true knowledge, not eating the apple. Lying is important, powerful and necessary, but has profound consequences in the intimacy of love. While the freedom to lie leads to power, the transparency of truth leads to intimacy. We need both truth and lies. The art is in knowing when to say which and to whom.

In intimate relationships we need the honesty of self-revelation, otherwise the love is not real. Love between two fantasies cannot remain alive, as love is nourished by reality not dreams, however subtle the lighting. This does not mean that to be honest we must relentlessly reveal the truth, since we rarely know what the truth is anyway, especially in the complicated inner terrain of intimate sexual love. Honesty lies in a willingness to enter an exploration to *discover* the truth. And truth, like language, has many faces.

Honesty does not mean you say everything. It is honest, for example, to say 'I do not want to tell you', or 'I don't trust you enough to share myself, or 'I'm too afraid to be honest'. You can then explore what lies behind the statement and discover the

CHAPTER TEN
The Truth Lies Between the Lies

I came and sat in front of you
as I would at an altar.
Every promise I made before
I broke when I saw you.
RUMI

Honest dialogue is the currency of intimacy and leads to a mutual inter-penetration of worlds. Without it we would neither meet nor understand each other. Honest communication is absolutely essential for making love. It builds bridges across the great divides that separate us, though bridges can be built in many different ways.

We use language to give information and make observations, establish contact, explore differences and common ground, build rapport and mutual empathy, give orders and directions, establish control, tell stories, express ourselves, release inner tensions, advise, share wisdom and experience, gossip, create poetry, songs, literature and theatre, celebrate rituals, invoke gods, pray, deceive, manipulate and lie.

In intimate relationships we do all of these, though not necessarily at the same time as our partners. Many arguments are the result of us using language differently.

A man returned from work and told his partner: 'I'm tired, I've had a hard day at work.' The woman said: 'So did I. It's hard out there.' He was hurt and felt she didn't care about him. He had wanted her to make him a cup of tea and listen to his tales of the office. She was offering empathy, letting him know that she knew how he felt.

A woman returned from work and told her partner: 'I'm tired, I had a hard day at work.' The man said: 'You can always leave and find another job. I saw one advertised you might like.' She was hurt and felt he didn't care about her. She had wanted him to sit with her and be sensitive to how she was feeling. He wanted to give her practical help so that she would not be tired in the future.

One of the most common misunderstandings between partners occurs when one is using language as a tool to work out what needs to be done, and the other is using language to create rapport and connection. Then we can feel divided by a common language. We understand the words, and think the meaning is clear, when the reality is very different.

The art of verbal communication lies in being able to link words and meaning. Apart from the fact this has challenged some of the world's greatest philosophers, it is not easy because words are powerful and are as often used to hide the truth as to reveal it. And, anyway, it is often not what we say, but the way we say it, that matters. The Finnish people, reputed to be the least talkative people in the world, have a proverb: 'One word is enough to make a lot of trouble'. But even silence can cause trouble between lovers.

We have the meaning of the message, the medium of the message and the meaning of the medium of the message

Not only are there many ways of using language, there are also many languages. Only a fraction of our communications is mediated by verbal language, particularly in intimate relationships. Our communications are through feeling, emotional expression, silence, energy, behaviour, body movements, dance, rituals, symbols and the inarticulate speech of the heart – each a different language – as well as through speech, dialogue, explanation, grammatical sentences, quotations, shouts, word play, hints and rhetoric. It is an achievement that we understand each other at all.

Zen stories are rarely about relationships. They tend to be more concerned with detachment, witnessing and aloneness than with communication, passion and intimacy. But this one appears to be also a parable for relationships.

There was a small Zen monastery with just two monks, who were brothers. The older was wise, learned and very saintly, while the younger was foolish, not very learned and only had one eye. One evening, very late, a traveller arrived. Zen monasteries have a tradition that any traveller can stay overnight if they win a debate with one of its monks. The older monk usually conducted these debates, but this night he was tired and so asked his younger brother to do it for him, but saying: 'Since you are so foolish, suggest that the debate be held in silence'. So the younger brother went to greet the traveller and suggested the debate be without words. The traveller agreed and they began.

Just as the older monk was climbing into his bed there came a knock at his door. In came the traveller, bowing. 'I had to come and thank you for the opportunity of debating with your most wise and learned brother. His depth of understanding of holy scriptures is so

profound, I count it a privilege to have lost the debate. You must be honoured to share a monastery with him.' The older monk raised an eyebrow and asked what had happened.

'Well first, your learned brother asked that the debate be in silence. Of course! The deepest truths cannot be communicated through words, only in silence. I knew immediately I was in the presence of a master. I then held up one finger to represent the truth of Buddha, whereupon your brother held up two fingers to represent the truth of Buddha and the commune around Buddha. I then held up three fingers to represent the truth of Buddha, his commune and the ultimate truth of all life, whereupon your brother held up no fingers at all to represent the essential unity of all things and the illusion of separation. I bowed down in defeat against such overwhelming brilliance. Thank you again.' And he walked off into the night to sleep under the stars.

Just as the older monk was climbing into bed again, in rushed his younger brother. 'That scoundrel! If I get my hands on him I'll beat him to a pulp! I have never met such a rude man in all my life!' The older monk raised his other eyebrow and asked what had happened.

'Well, I did as you suggested and asked that the debate be in silence. He then held up one finger to show that I only had one eye. I, being polite, held up two fingers to show that he had two eyes. Whereupon he, the wretch, held up three fingers to show that we had only three eyes between us! So I shook my fist in his face and he ran off!'

The body of love in a relationship can translate and mediate

In the intense intimacy of sexual relationships, where there are only the two of you, and with so many multimedia languages, messages and meanings, there are plenty of opportunities 'for misunderstanding'. A translator is often needed that understands both languages. This is yet another situation where we need our love.

When each of you communicates to the body of your love, to the relationship rather than directly to each other, some communications become much easier. There is less need to worry about your partner's reactions, that they may be hurt or angry with what you are saying, as the love in the relationship takes care of them. Neither will you be judged or rejected for what you reveal, as the body of your love will do neither. If you or your partner do reject what the other says, then this becomes pa

hidden reasons for saying it, or you can just leave it as it is, a simple statement of fact. But this does not undermine love. The truth *never* does this.

Even a lie can point to the truth

Lies are often seen as a betrayal of trust, but it is more important to find the meaning of a lie than to condemn it. And, anyway, we all lie when we don't know the truth, and often the truth is we don't know that we are lying. This is often the case between sexual partners, as so much of what is really going on is at the deep instinctual levels, within the energy of the body, way below consciousness.

If our partners lie to us, as well as dealing with our hurt and anger, we need to uncover the dynamic that led to the lie. Linking into the relationship is very useful here as it supports an exploration of why the lie happened. Has the one who was lied to refused to hear the truth for so long that their partner has given up trying to tell them? Has the one who was lied to become an emotional bully who kicks up when hearing things they do not like? Are they lying in another arena, and this lie provides the balance? Have tyrannical religious or political beliefs made the truth hide? Has lying become a habitual protection for the one who has lied? Do they feel the truth cannot be spoken? Are they lying because of a childhood fear that needs to be understood rather than judged? Was the lie a mistaken way of trying to take care? Are they hiding from a sense of shame that the condemnation of the lie is only making worse? Is the truth too threatening?

A Linking exercise that helps is to sit facing your love-body saying whatever you both want to about the lie and the situation that gave rise to it. After 10 minutes both close your eyes and be silent for five minutes. Then talk to your love-body for another 10 minutes, followed by another five minutes with your eyes closed and in silence. Continue periods of talking followed by periods of silence for as long as you have agreed. In the silence notice any ideas, thoughts, sensations or feelings that come to you.

What is the truth and what is a lie is rarely simple. Revealing yourself can be a deception anyway when a deeper truth is that you want to lie. And there are many ways to communicate the truth whatever our words might be.

For many years a woman would be furious with her partner whenever he lied during their arguments. She would say 'But you promised . . .', and he would say 'No I didn't', even when he knew he had. Or, 'You can't really mean you're leaving!' 'Yes I do', when he was only saying it to upset her. She believed that they must speak the truth to each other and stood by this herself. She felt hurt when he lied, as well as angry. Finally, they sat together to explore this difference as a problem they both had, since they knew that if one was hurt and angry, this involved them both.

They began to look together for the hidden symmetry that they knew would be found somewhere in their relationship. If he was lying, in what way was she? This was difficult because she was so committed to telling the truth. And then it hit her. She lied many times behaviourally. She would sometimes smile when she felt angry, or appear rational and calm when she really wanted to scream. He never lied in this way. She always knew how he was feeling, anyone could – it would be written all over him. Strangely enough, as soon as she realised this, in the synchronous magic of a relationship, he stopped lying, too. He would only lie anyway when she was demanding he explain himself. Why had he done it? What for? What was his real motivation? What was he unconsciously trying to do? This barrage of questions while appearing to her perfectly reasonable was also a way of getting at him. He would then protect himself by shouting and saying anything that came into his head, irrespective of whether he thought it true or not. He couldn't win through words because she had more power there. But shouting, that was a different matter. He felt safer in this territory and would therefore try to wrestle the fights into the realm of energy while she would try to wrestle it back into language.

Most of our communications hide the truth rather than reveal it

Honest communication involves us being vulnerable to the truth in sexual, emotional and spiritual dialogues. In other words, we do not restrict the communication to solely the areas where we feel safe, perhaps being polite at the expense of being real, keeping quiet to keep the peace, and intellectualising rather than feeling. Real communication means being willing to be truthful even when our partners want to explore something that threatens us.

Observations of communications within families have revealed there are basically five forms of communication:

1 Placating – keeping it nice, being subservient.
2 Blaming – attacking, criticising.
3 Intellectualisation – detached analysis, meaning observations that are

disconnected from feeling.

4   Distracting – irrelevancies, telling stories.

5   Direct – honest, truthful, real.

All but the last are ways in which we disengage from honest dialogue when we feel threatened. Less than 1% of the communications observed were direct, honest and real. 99% were in some way avoiding reality. Love needs us to be real more than it needs us to be caring, sensitive, empathic, funny, assertive, articulate, clever, original, witty, clear, emotional or rational. So what does this say about the way we are nurturing love in our families and intimate relationships?

To feed love, honesty is essential, even when our partners are not. However afraid, uncomfortable, ashamed or anxious we might be, if we are sincere in our attempts to be honest, then in the symmetry of relationships this is the best way to encourage our partners also to be honest. If your partner persists in lying, then you may well ask yourself why you are with them. There will be a reason, and if your commitment to the truth is real, you will find it. By knowing this you can then make a conscious choice about what to do.

Dialogue involves standing your ground while being willing to give way

There are two ways to nurture dialogue:

- We enter the other's world and listen to them from there.
- We are resolutely honest irrespective of the effect of this honesty on the other.

Both are needed.

The first, empathy, involves an exploration of how the other experiences things. We put ourselves into the other's shoes and attempt to see through their eyes, getting a sense of what it is like to be them. We become sensitive to subtle signals from our partners about things they may not even be aware of themselves. Through this we can understand better what is important to our partners, what they need, and how to communicate in ways they can understand. Without a degree of empathy for the other, there can be no real communication.

The second, honesty, requires us to remain connected with ourselves and not to allow considerations for our partners to distract us from our own experience. Standing our ground while facing our partners, though it makes us vulnerable, is also what gives us authority and presence. This is the other pole, essential for building bridges. A bridge needs two poles to support it. Without a genuine transparency and honesty, there is not enough of us entering the picture. And there is no relationship without us.

Most of us tend to be more familiar with one of these modes than the other. And since opposites attract, each seeking the energies and skills they lack, we tend to be drawn to those who manifest the opposite energetic pole to ourselves. It is useful to practise being the pole you are less at ease with, as it is a powerful tool for a relationship when each partner can be both empathic and honest.

One way to develop empathy for each other's position is to play out everyday scenes together where you swap roles. Especially useful is to play a familiar recurring argument. This can be done in the middle of a heated fight or later, when things have cooled somewhat – both can be helpful. There are some exercises at the end of this chapter that help the development of empathy between you.

To bring yourself more into the picture, make statements with 'I' in them, especially if you generally communicate using 'you' or 'we'. 'I don't like this' is more real than 'you shouldn't be doing this' or 'we agreed this was not a good idea'.

True dialogue is a journey into the unknown

Honest dialogue is definitely not easy. We are exposed and vulnerable, and because we have dared to reveal ourselves and have been honest, we can be rejected, attacked, ignored, laughed at, humiliated and judged.

Socrates gave birth to the spirit of dialogue. He was the first man to claim that truth could be discovered by each of us in creative dialogue with each other and not only through divine revelation. He challenged what was then assumed to be the very nature of human communication and language and explored dialogue as a method of exploration for ideas and discovery. Before this, speech and conversation had been functional ('Pass the salt'), or rhetorical ('We are the salt of the earth'). There was no meaningful conversation to explore reality. People would debate with each other, making statements in monologues, declaiming what they thought to be true, arguing their position and taking a stand. Your 'opponent' would similarly pronounce on things from where they stood. You either won the argument and were right, or lost it and were wrong. Like enemies on a battlefield or tribes at war, the victorious won the lot. This is not a good recipe for intimate communication between lovers.

In dialogue, we listen to what the other is saying and are more interested in discovering the truth than in winning the argument. Socrates would use questions to draw the other out, to enable them to articulate their thoughts with increasing subtlety and intricacy as the dialogue continued. Using the insights and experiences of each, the partners in dialogue would evolve between them a deeper understanding than either would have reached separately. Socrates described it as using dialogue to give birth to new thoughts. Understandings and ideas were born out of the relationships between the people, rather than the survival of the fittest in a war of beliefs and dogmas. It is interesting that Socrates was also the first person to define love as a human mystery and not an affliction from the gods. And, like so many who have dared to claim the power of gods as belonging to us, bringing to earth and making human what had previously lived only in heaven, he was put to death.

Despite thousands of years since the Socratic Dialogues appeared, many of us still haven't learned the art of dialogue. We want to be right more than we want to know, we want to be seen as knowing rather than not knowing, we get off on rhetoric rather than inquiry, we want to win the argument rather than find the truth, and we prefer to defend our position than learn something new. Nowhere do we do this more than in arguments with our partners. Dialogue brings us face to face with the truth of ourselves and our partners, and although we may not like what we find, the intimacy that results from being real together is so good that we end up wanting to be honest more than we want to hide behind lies. At least, that is what our love will try to persuade us to do.

True love loves the truth

We owe those who have had the courage to love us at least the truth of ourselves, even if that truth is not what they want. The conflict between not wanting to hurt the other's feelings and yet also wanting to be honest is one most of us encounter. Only experience can teach us when we are hiding the truth because we are afraid of the consequences of revealing ourselves, or because we are genuinely caring for someone. And even then the truth will have to be told that we do not want to tell them the truth and do not know why. To find true love, we must love the truth.

One of the most painful experiences we can have with someone we love is when the full truth of what we know and feel cannot be spoken because there is no space to receive it.

> A woman and a man had been together for many years. Maybe something went awry years previously and had not been not dealt with and digested. Maybe the fulfillment of their love required this process. Who knows? But the woman fell in with a group of people gathered around a charismatic leader who was teaching a powerful transformational process leading to 'spiritual enlightenment'. The process demanded a level of commitment that meant daily care for their children, and making money became secondary. The woman

believed that the search for enlightenment was more important than the family, and that the children needed an enlightened mother more than they needed her, imperfect as she was, and the security of home and routine. The man knew this was not the case. He knew this from his own experience, not prejudiced judgment, as before they had met he had gone on a similar spiritual journey. He had learned many important things, including the importance and power of love in everyday life.

The woman thought the man was stubbornly refusing to see the truth of what her guru was teaching. She became increasingly angry and frustrated and eventually left. The man could do nothing but take care of the children and feel the loss. He knew how impossible it is to dissuade someone who is so devoted to a cause that anything said would simply be interpreted as more resistance and refusal. Because he, too, had been there, he also knew that for this process to work for her, there had to be a complete surrender on her part. He could not explain all this to her as she would not understand. There was nothing to do but allow the process to unfold.

The body of their love, however, was strong enough for both of them to be able to genuinely say that if they were meant to come back together, then they would. If not, then so be it. But love's wisdom did not make the heartbreak any less.

Love deals in reality not dreams

Having honest communication and therefore real intimacy makes love. It creates an energy field around the couple that further makes each of them love. Over time, this energy field becomes a body of love with the power to bring things into form, to make things happen in their lives. It grows into a greater power than anything they have known before, but it does not prevent the reality of suffering. Love is about reality, not happiness, and true happiness can only be found in reality. Love will rescue us from the tyranny of even our sweetest dreams, to show us the deeper goodness in reality.

This man suffered the loss of his wife, his love in this particular form, this person. He did not, however, suffer the loss of his love. His love did not die but lived on in the way he did not attack her, interfere with her freedom and, perhaps most important of all, in any way undermine her relationship with the children. This love in him would in time draw towards him another form, another person, with whom he could manifest and express his love. Love is the most primal and powerful of magics, drawing into form again and again aspects of the formless, incorporating energies so that we can know love in this most basic level of reality, the material. And who knows? For this man it may be again the same woman, who having learned whatever lessons were there for her with her guru, returns home. When Buddha himself returned home after seven years seeking enlightenment, he was met by his wife who, hurt by his absence, asked: 'If what you have found is the universal truth, why could you not have found it here with me?' He replied: 'I had to leave in order to discover there was no need to leave.'

That the children had a father with such a wise love is perhaps a greater gift than even parents who stay together. So, in a way the woman was right, too. Children need an evolved wisdom somewhere in their lives. Maybe she was right in another way, too. Her journey with this guru may be exactly what was required by their love to counterbalance her partner's greater wisdom and experience, especially if he had assumed a teaching/therapist role with her, not appropriate for the balance in the later years of their marriage. This separation may be a vital stage in their journey together. It's not over until both sing.

True communication involves our bodies, hearts, minds and spirits

Honest dialogue is difficult to begin with, but once you have begun to experience its benefits, you will not settle for less. It creates a place with your partner where everything can be shared without the fear of judgment or reprisal that you would encounter if you tried it elsewhere. A restaurant will not appreciate you sitting and weeping into the soup, nor a board meeting want to hear about your frustrations at home, but with your partner you can slowly develop a trust in which you can share everything. As you practise honest dialogue with your partner, you will feel increasingly safe to be yourself. You will begin to trust the relationship deeply. You will allow your partner into the dark corners of your psyche, which may have been hidden away from love for a very long time. Love can then reach the parts that need love the most. You will discover fresh aspects of yourself and your partner continually. And once you begin honest dialogue with your partner, beginning an endlessly revealing journey into the unknown, you will not want to stop.

Communication Exercises

Here are some suggestions to help establish communication and create dialogue between you.

1. To understand emotional communication you need to *feel* what your partner is feeling, not merely listen to what they are saying. Practise feeling them

emotionally, by closing your eyes and sensing them. You'll learn to feel your partner's subtle energies and feelings, as well as attuning to energy generally. Don't wait for an argument to do this.

2. Try doing this in bed when you are lying in each other's arms. Let the feelings you have and any pictures or odd stray thoughts give you information about what is happening between you on levels other than your mind.

3. Share whatever comes to you, however trivial, silly or crazy you might think it is. A dialogue that begins 'I dont know why but I suddenly remembered when you broke your leg', is more likely to yield a new understanding than 'Why did you do that?'.

4. Have an argurment without words.

5. One of you makes a statement – for instance, 'I am thirsty'. The other asks a series of questions beginning with 'Do you mean . . . ?'. For example, 'Do you mean you want me to open a bottle of wine?', 'Do you mean you're upset that I haven't offered you any tea?', and 'Do you mean you need me?'. You keep asking until you receive four replies of 'Yes'. This helps you learn about the hidden agendas in seemingly simple statements, since even the one speaking will often not know what they mean immediately.

6. You each tell a story from your childhood, giving only the facts. The other listens and when you have finished shares how they imagine you felt and what has been the effect of that incident or experience in the way you live your life. This works best if it is a strong formative experience you are describing.

7. You each tell a story from your childhood, this time including whatever you wish to say. The other listens without saying anything and then shares what they think you left out of the account. Again, you will be learning the significance of the unspoken.

8. Work out which one of you has the greater power of the word, and how the other maintains the balance of power, perhaps by walking away, shouting, being funny, attacking, or pretending to be busy with other things.

9. Have an argument where the one with the greater word power cannot speak but can move and make noises, and the other can speak but not move or make noises.

10. One takes a particular behaviour in their partner that really irritates, upsets or hurts them, and asks their partner questions about this behaviour that can only be answered 'Yes' or 'No'. For example, if one walks out of the room during an argument and this infuriates the other, then that partner should ask: 'Do you do this to hurt me?', 'Do you know why you do it?', 'Would you like to find another way of behaving?', 'Does it feel as if this is all you can do?', 'Are you afraid if you stay you'll say or do something destructive?'. Continue with this until the partner

asking the questions has received sufficient 'Yes' replies for them to feel they understand the meaning of what the other one is doing. You then change over.

11. Every now and then declare war on each other and sit with your love as mediator while you pour it all out – not to each other, but to your love, referring to each other by name or 'he' or 'she'. This allows things to be said that might otherwise fester, and brings to the surface what needs to come to light. Don't rush off to a dinner party straight after, but take time to care for the vulnerability that will also emerge. The care you take of each other after an argument is very important for healing past wounds as well as present ones.

12. Whenever you are convinced you are right, try assuming you're wrong.

13. Tell the truth to each other, which may be 'I do not want to tell you the truth'.

14. Sit side by side facing your love, the body of the relationship, and allow each to speak to it for five minutes exactly in turn. Neither interrupts, says anything or asks questions while the other is speaking. You can blame, judge, play victim and refuse to take responsibility, or you can be as enlightened, compassionate and as unconditionally accepting as you wish. You also have the right to remain silent, withdrawn and stubborn. The structure holds you while you are free to say whatever you wish. Give this a long time so that the river first begins to flow and then the currents can take you into whatever deep waters are revealed. Then dive into them.

15. Do everything you can to reach a transparent honesty between you, while knowing you will always remain essentially unknowable mysteries to each other.

CHAPTER ELEVEN

Love is in the Detail

A night full of talking that hurts,
my worst held-back secrets: Everything
has to do with loving and not loving.
This night will pass,
Then we have work to do.
RUMI

A research project examined the lives of successful people in many walks of life, including entrepreneurs, lawyers, people in business, politics, creative artists, musicians and writers, to find out what made them successful. Three factors were found. The first was daring to have a big vision, the second was persistence, the third was attention to detail.

In our culture we tend to have a pretty big vision for our love affairs – that they will bring happiness and love into our lives, that we will live together forever in harmony, and that we will never do anything to hurt the one we love. So there's no problem with the vision, it seems. We also tend to be persistent. After a love affair is over, even if we have had our heart broken, one day we usually fall in love again. On average, we each have twelve relationships before we marry, and most people who divorce will marry again. So there's no difficulty, on the whole, with persistence then. The third factor, however, is frequently a problem. We do not pay enough attention to the details.

Many fights have their origins in hurts that have been ignored

There is a tendency in most of us to brush aside irrational and awkward feelings, often because we don't want to rock the boat and are afraid of appearing petty and foolish and disturbing the peace. Yet wars begin long before they are declared, and most arguments in a relationship begin with a minor irritation, a slight hurt, an unattended detail.

A says to B: 'The window needs closing'. B closes it but feels irritated, and then guilty for feeling this. The window does not actually need closing. The window does not need anything. A simply wants it to be closed and seems to expect someone else to do it. Perhaps A has a difficulty in expressing a need without also controlling what happens. Perhaps A often projects their own needs onto others. Perhaps it is a way of manipulating the other without revealing anything of themselves. Whatever is the hidden dynamic here, it will surface continually in the relationship until it is dealt with and digested, as love will continually bring out whatever may be blocking the flow of love.

Meanwhile, B's instincts know something is not quite right but not exactly what, and so cannot articulate it. B doesn't trust their instincts, buries the irritation and then feels guilty. This guilt will not just disappear. It will slowly accumulate until one day it either explodes in an attack on A – 'You never do anything for yourself. You're always telling me what to do!' – or takes them away from A – 'My partner doesn't understand me, they just use me'.

A couple plan a holiday. C says: 'I don't want to go anywhere hot.' D says: 'Oh, but you'll love Thailand, it's so exotic.' C goes along with it because D is so happy to go and C doesn't want to cause trouble. But there's trouble anyway.

C hates the heat, and they have a miserable time and many arguments. Both had been working hard and wanted a good holiday, and while both had done their best to make this happen, they had failed. Important details were missed. C needs to share more of how she really feels, while D needs to listen. This drama will be played out in different forms again and again, in increasingly painful scenarios, until they turn around and consciously address it. If they don't, this could threaten the whole relationship.

One says: 'I'm really worried about what people will think of me.' The other, trying to help, says: 'Don't be silly, it doesn't matter. You're fine.' The first, having been often told as a child she was silly, keeps their fears to themselves in future. The second thinks it's all OK. But it isn't.

We are not responsible for what we feel, only for what we do

In loving relationships everything matters. Even apparently small details are important. The sooner we deal with things, the less entrenched is the difficulty and the easier the resolution. Love is undermined when we ignore difficulties, conflicts, hurts and angers, brushing these feelings under the carpet, hoping they'll go away or sort themselves out. They never do. They will accumulate out of sight and out of mind until one day we find they have built into great divides that threaten the whole relationship. And no-one knows what is really going on or why.

We might fear that anger, irritation, boredom, criticism, need, fear, hate, judgment, alienation, etc, undermine love, but they do not. Ignoring these feelings, however, will. Feelings are naturally-occurring phenomena, like the weather. They are happenings, not things we do. What we feel in any situation is our natural response to life through our particular genetic, social, psychological, spiritual heritage. We are not responsible for *what* we feel, only for what we *do*. The fact we are angry, sad or sexually attracted to someone who is not our partner is not something we can be blamed for – it is simply a fact of life. What matters is what we do about it. Do we, for example, let our fear control us? Or do we feel our fear and do it anyway, or not, as the situation demands or we decide?

> *A couple went to relationship counselling. 'He is so angry all the time. He shouts at me and the children. He storms out when I try to talk to him. He leaps up and bangs the table and frightens us all. He's always frowning.' 'She's always moaning and complaining. She's never happy. Nothing I do satisfies her. There's always something wrong in her opinion.' The sessions continued for weeks with her complaining about his anger and his getting angry with her complaints. Nothing seemed to be shifting until I suggested to them that they swap roles and play each other. They rose to the occasion. The woman leaped up shouting, banging on the table, threatening to hit the other or walk out. The man wailed into a tissue: 'Oh poor me – you don't understand me, you're so cruel and horrid, life is so terrible living with you.' After a while it became clear that they were enjoying this. Or rather, they were enjoying being able to react to each other in a different way. They both came alive.*
>
> *They agreed to sit side by side, linking into their love for a period of time each day. The man was to express his anger and the woman her distress and then they would switch roles for a while. Then they were to close their eyes and sit in silence holding each other's hand, creating a connection with their love beyond this dynamic. This exercise was giving them each an opportunity to express their anger and complaint, to get a perspective on what they were doing through hearing the other, to connect with other energies than the ones they were familiar with and to be together with their love. This simple exercise turned everything around. Without any particular awareness or conscious exploration of the relationship, what had been spiralling further into trouble became gradually lighter.*

This man and woman made linking in and sharing how they felt with the body of their love part of their daily routine, like having a shower. Even when there were no problems, it seemed to keep them fluid and connected with their love in ways that worked for them.

If you feel hurt by your partner and keep it to yourself, you in turn hurt the relationship

If you do not let your partner know when you feel hurt by them, the hurts accumulate and, slowly but surely, this takes you away from them. Every hurt needs to be attended to, as it is a sign that something needs to be taken care of in the relationship. Never, therefore, ignore either your own hurt or your partner's. When your partner says they feel hurt by you, then you may well feel angry, irritated or annoyed, but you must deal with it. You do not have to feel compassionate or caring. This might mean you express how irritated you feel, that you wish they would just shut up and relax, chill and stop moaning. One way to do this in a less threatening way is through a Linking exercise where you both moan and complain about each other to the love-body of the relationship. Apart from letting off some steam, a deeper reality will eventually reveal itself. The important thing is to deal with it and be honest. If you don't, it's like ignoring a pain in the body – you run the risk of serious disease setting in.

What we fight about is usually symbolic of something deeper

Chronic disagreements always point to a hidden deeper dynamic. Arguments about money, for example, are rarely about money per se, but more about what the money symbolises. Money means different things to different people. It might mean security to one and freedom to another, or status to one and a burden to another. The arguments may be using money as a symbol for these other differences.

'You're so mean' can mean 'I need more freedom'. 'You should stop spending so much' can mean 'I need you'. These meta-messages (the hidden messages behind the surface of what is being said), are hard to decipher as often neither one knows these deeper currents. However, arguing endlessly about money when the real dynamic is something different will get nowhere.

Linking helps as the non-threatening atmosphere created by sharing differences with our love allows these hidden meanings to emerge. Like wild animals who only emerge from hiding when it is safe, the deeper realities of our fears will only be spoken when there's a safe place to receive them. Even small details about housekeeping – who opens the bank statements, and where the cheque books are kept – can have important meanings if arguments about money feature in your relationship.

Similarly, arguments about family or who does what in the house are often codes referring to more intimate troubles that cannot be easily put into words.

A couple lived far from both their families and would argue each year about whose parents they would visit at Christmas. The man argued that they should go to his parents as he was their only child and they were getting old. The woman argued that her sisters and brothers all lived around her parents and this way she could see them all together. And besides, their children would have more fun playing with their cousins, and they could visit his parents anytime. Every year they would end up going to the woman's family. Eventually the man's parents died and there were no more fights about this.

Twenty years later they came to counselling. The man had told the woman he wanted a divorce in order to marry another woman with whom he had been having an affair for four years. This woman had become pregnant and he now wanted to marry her. He had agreed to counselling, even though his mind was made-up, hoping to ease the anguish and pain of his wife during the separation. She came hoping to fix it between them and that he would stay with her. These different agendas needed to be fully acknowledged by both before any form of dialogue could begin. Despite the man's expressing repeatedly and clearly what he wanted, it was very difficult for the woman to take it on board. She decided to come for some sessions alone to explore in depth her deep and painful feelings of betrayal, anger and hurt about what had happened.

She discovered that there had been many clues as to what had been going on but that she had turned away, not wanting to face the possibility of her husband having an affair. She began to digest the truth of their life together. During this time, the man left and the divorce proceedings began. She continued in counselling and discovered that she had never really left her family of origin. Although she was married she had remained more a daughter to her parents than a wife to her husband. She had taken her children into her original family, rather than creating her own family. This had deprived her husband of her primary loyalty, his position as father and his authority and power as provider for the children. That she had never left her first family also meant that she had not really opened to his family and had had no feeling for his parents' loneliness or vulnerability. She saw how much this all had wounded the relationship with her husband beyond repair, and how he had therefore sought to create another family that was his. The arguments about Christmas had really been about far more, though neither knew this at the time. Her deep sorrow for what had happened eventually dissolved all her bitterness and she became a wise woman.

She moved back to live near her extended family. She never remarried but became a source of support and wisdom for her many brothers, sisters, nephews and nieces, as well as her own children and grandchildren. And she was loved by them all in return. She became especially good at noticing the small details before they grew into great problems.

We need arguments about details to help uncover the real difficulties

We naturally try to resolve disagreements through rational discussion, but conflict in sexual relationships usually has its roots in the irrational and instinctive, which means we need different ways to find out what is needed than would be appropriate at work or in other less emotionally charged situations. Acknowledging that fights with partners usually have their source in the hidden undercurrents of the relationship, and are not only about the issues being argued about, is very important. For a start, it leads to an exploration of what really needs to be addressed, though this is hard to do in the heat and passion of a fight.

There are four steps involved in uncovering what underlies a recurring argument:

1   Don't dismiss the fight as trivial or unimportant.
2   Acknowledge you do not know what the fight is really about, and be willing to find out.
3   Listen to thoughts and feelings that might easily be dismissed as 'petty' or 'silly'.
4   Find out what your behaviour is saying, not only what your words are.

Let us look at each of these in turn.

1. Pay attention to the small things

When our love is trying to draw attention to deeper issues than we are aware of, then arguments *have* to begin with some concrete, but maybe apparently trivial, detail. There is no other way. If we knew what was going on, we would be halfway to resolving it and not bogged down in disagreements and fights in the first place. It is often only through disagreements about specific behaviour that we can tap into what is going on at a deeper level. It is easy to dismiss trivial details such as leaving clothes lying around, the way you greet each other, how you eat, who holds the TV control, not cleaning the bath, and forgetting to put out the rubbish, but no detail is too trivial for love. And if the arguments recur, we must deal with them sooner or later – better sooner.

2. Not knowing allows more exploration than knowing

Most of us think that not to know what is going on is somehow a failing. Certainly, this happens at school, and so as not to appear stupid we pretend or imagine we know. This can keep an argument going at a superficial level – who does the ironing? – rather than engaging in whatever is the real power battle. Acknowledging that neither knows the real reason for the conflict is an important step in resolving it.

This is particularly important if either of you is convinced you are right. A useful Linking exercise here involves sitting side by side facing the body of the relationship and saying in turns whatever you wish to, but beginning by saying: '(She/he is right, and . . . ', even when you don't actually believe your partner is right at all. For example, you might say: 'He is right and I think his suggestion is stupid and not going to work at all, but he won't listen to me'. Or, 'She is right and she doesn't understand what I'm saying at all and just dismisses it'. And so on, back and forth. It soon becomes apparent that both of you are right, and an understanding is needed that includes both positions.

3. The irrational is very insightful, the instinctive very intelligent

Once we acknowledge that we do not know the real reason for the argument, the next step involves becoming co-detectives, though this investigation may take some time, even years, to complete. The final resolution of many deeper conflicts can only be found when enough love has been made to embrace all aspects of both poles. And this takes time, as major conflicts, as we have seen, have their roots in personal histories, events earlier in the relationship, cultural issues and collective existential aspects of life, as well as the immediate.

To explore these deeper currents, we need our intuition and instincts. The details of specific arguments are like the ends of a piece of string in a complex tangle – to untangle the string we must first find an end. One way to do this is to sit together facing the love-body of the relationship and share any pictures that come to you and any dreams you may have. Pay attention to any small feelings of irritation, hurt, boredom and anxiety. Share any stray thought that may seem irrelevant, as well as odd memories, hopes and fears. Try doing this, too, with your eyes closed, just saying what comes to you without any analysis or comment. After 10 minutes or so, talk about what has been said and see if you can get a sense of what it all might mean.

Jung used to say that to analyse dreams you should place them in the centre of the room and walk around them, letting the dream reveal itself bit by bit. You can do this with your dreams and other thoughts and feelings by placing them in front of your love and simply waiting. In time, what is important will be revealed to you.

4. We need to learn the language of behaviour

The spoken word is not really designed to communicate the irrational and instinctive, and since the currency of emotional intimacy is the flow of feeling, verbal language is limited. As a consequence we tend to express our frustration and suffering in the relationship by complaining about something more concrete, such as the washing-up. If we don't share the small things that bother us, the irritations that we can brush aside because we think they are silly or keep quiet about to keep the peace, then we miss what may be the first hint of something very significant. Vague uncomfortable feelings about something going on in the relationship are very hard to articulate, and often reveal themselves more easily in an irrational reaction to the way our partners breathe or drink, or the clothes they wear, or some other small habit of theirs.

A woman had many lovers. As soon as her lovers wanted a more committed relationship, she began to feel irritated with them and left. Eventually she became engaged to a man. Six weeks before the wedding everything about the man began to annoy her. All his faults became magnified and he appeared to her as a wimp, a failure, a pathetic character who would never amount to much. She did not hold back criticising him and telling him how she felt. He was confused and hurt, which infuriated her even more.

One day her mother heard her going on at him and told her: 'I think you've got pre-wedding nerves'. The woman stopped. This had never occurred to her. Her mother went on to explain how she, too, had nearly walked away from her own wedding through exactly this kind of rejection of her fiance. 'But your grandmother told me it was just nerves. And so it was.' It was a shock to the woman that her strong feelings could really be her fear of commitment.

In previous relationships her love had not been greater than her fear. This time it was. After she married, the security of the commitment proved to be exactly what she had been looking for all her life without realising it. Underneath all her criticisms and irritations she had been afraid and craving the very security she was rejecting.

It can take many years for love to reveal what is really going on underneath the kinds of misunderstandings and irritations around everyday things such as being late, forgetting to put sugar in our tea, and leaving towels on the floor. Yet if they are indicative of some deeper imbalance that needs addressing, then the energy field of the love in the relationship will keep bringing them to the surface to be dealt with.

Often, the reason we fight about details is because the hidden hurt is hard to articulate. We simply do not know what it is, as it is below our consciousness. Even very profound issues usually reveal themselves initially through some small upset about, say, the way we were asked to close a window or open a door. So when you feel hurt, resentful, guilty, afraid or unhappy, even when it's so slight you feel embarrassed to bring it up, make sure you tell your partner about it. Saying 'I don't feel right and don't know why' is more productive and encourages an exploration; saying nothing does nothing. It is easier to hear our partners telling us they have trouble with the way we ask for things than it is to hear years later that they are fed-up with being treated like a slave and are never going to do anything for us again.

Suggestions to help you deal with fights before they grow into great conflicts

1   At the end of the day or on an evening walk, go over your day together, noticing anything that may have been a problem for you, however slight.

2   If you find yourself thinking about something several days after it has happened, go back to your partner and share it.

3   If something felt different or strange while making love, or if you feel worried or disturbed in any way, talk about it as soon as possible.

4   While out together, or with the children, or in the workplace, you may be sharp with each other or abrupt. Later, when there is time and privacy, talk about it. Sort it out – don't leave it.

5   Have a private code you can use in public that signals to each other that you have noticed something has upset one of you and that you agree to deal with it later. The agreement provides support in that moment, even if you cannot deal with the upset immediately.

6   If either approaches the other with something, however irritated and frustrated the other is, then agree to deal with it, if possible at an agreed time so that both are prepared for it.

7   In an evening, when the children are in bed, sometimes ignore daily habits such as putting the TV on or playing music to simply be together without these usual distractions.

8 If you find yourself doing DIY, cooking, gardening, or whatever, and somehow it does not feel right, or you feel vaguely upset, find out with your partner what is really going on. Don't always wait for a good moment, as sometimes now, however inconvenient, is the best time to deal with things.

Dealing with the detail of relationship is not easy. For example, going back to deal with yesterday, last week or last year, opposes a cultural tendency to go forwards, to progress towards the goal in the future. It is also difficult as we have expectations and images from the media that edits out boring, problematic, irritating and awkward details. And although we know life is not like the movies, and the image is not the reality, the way that love is portrayed in the media does affect us. Also, we do not want to appear petty, awkward, silly, obsessed with trivia, uncool and neurotic when we focus on small hurts and slights. And then there is the simple fact that paying attention to the detail of life with our partners is hard work.

Yet we cannot make love without a body. And as soon as the reality of the body is involved, the details of a situation not only begin to matter, they *are* what is happening. As with our physical bodies, so it is with our love-bodies. Pay attention to the small things and the big things will look after themselves. What we eat, how we breathe, attending to a cut, and learning from small signals in the body all contribute more to our health than an annual check-up. Sharing when we feel hurt, talking about a small worry, going back over something vaguely disturbing, and saying something even when we don't know what it's about, all contribute more to keeping our love healthy than an annual holiday, where we hope the relaxation will do it for us.

Nothing is too small, too insignificant, too trivial or too unimportant for our love. Everything matters to love. Not only are God and the devil in the details – it seems love is, too.

THE SEXUALITY OF LOVE

CHAPTER TWELVE

The Spirituality of the Body

Remember. In the way you make love
is the way God will be with you.
RUMI

Sex is far more mysterious and complex than we realise. It is as much a mystery as love, life and death, and like all such unfathomable phenomena is a mystery to be lived rather than analysed or explained. Yet the sexuality of love is absolutely central to our human experience of life, and to understand love, we have to explore love's sexuality.

These next four chapters explore the sexuality of love. The first two look at the nature of sex and at the deeper spiritual meaning of human love. The next two deal with more practical aspects of sex and making love.

Sex is one of the facts of life on this planet

Life on this planet is sexual. So is love. Any ideas we may have of love that are not grounded in the realities of life, not rooted in the body, soon become unreal fantasies and die. Sex brings us back from virtual realities and dreams, and roots us back into the realities of the here and now – we wake up and smell a lot more than the coffee. And anyway, ideas cannot make love – only bodies can. Sex, like life and love, is beyond any of our ideas of it. It is as vast and varied as life itself.

It can make us feel like gods one moment – powerful, glorious, free and full of life – then raw, helpless, vulnerable and at the mercy of life in the next. We feel powerful because when sexual energy flows through our bodies, we feel full of life and released from inhibitions, self-doubt and awkwardness. We feel vulnerable because we open our deepest selves and allow another so close that we become utterly defenceless.

Sex is the natural heritage of every human being. Anyone alive can enjoy sex – you don't have to be rich or famous or clever or perfect. Sex can be a timeless meeting with someone we never meet again, or it can involve a lifelong commitment to knowing each other completely. It can be a play of the moment or a discovery over time. We can have candles and music, or darkness and silence. We can be streetwise and powerful or as innocent as a babe. We can let go and let it all happen, or choose to control things for a different pleasure. We can do anything or we can do nothing, and still we can make love.

Making love connects us with both our power and our vulnerability

Having sex and making love are not necessarily the same, however. Having sex involves the instincts of the body, but not the persons. We experience the impersonal energies of sex without the personal dimensions of a relationship. We do not, for example, have to deal with the personal conflicts and vulnerabilities that we all know so well in our intimate relationships, yet, as we have seen, it is through these very struggles that we create more love and understanding.

We make love through the intimacy created by our needs and vulnerabilities, not only through our powers and glories. Making love, therefore, involves the personal aspects of who and what we are. There is an old story that when God had finished making Adam and Eve, he invited the angels to view his latest creation. He told the angels to bow down before this man and woman. Lucifer, the greatest and brightest of all the angels, refused, saying he would bow down only to God, who alone was the source of all things. For this, Lucifer was expelled from heaven and became Satan.

This story shows how even with our human frailties and imperfection, we have a central role in the evolution of existence. Without our vulnerabilities, we could not make love. Gods, angels and deities, with all their powers and glories, on the other hand, are immortal – they cannot be mortally wounded, they do not die. They are, therefore, never vulnerable, and though they can love, they cannot make love. It seems the universe needs us, with our human needs, insecurities and vulnerabilities, to make the love that makes the world go round, that keeps the celestial spheres in motion, and that gives the spin to it all. And without the circular motion of heavenly bodies, the whole universe would implode.

The landscape of myth is the landscape of the human spirit. All of us are both Lucifer and Satan, angel and devil, proud and vulnerable, divine and animal. Sexual love, more than any other human activity, confronts us with these opposing polarities struggling within us, and challenges us to acknowledge both poles. And it does this intimately, intensely and relentlessly.

In this context, considerations of how often, what position, how many orgasms, what kind, whether we make a noise or are silent, keep the light on or do it in the dark, are all less important than whether we make love or not. If, while making love, we feel in love with our partners, then all the technique, multiple orgasms and sexual yoga in the world could not take us to a better place. And when lying in the arms of the one we love and who loves us, we know the pleasures of an intimacy that may make even angels jealous.

Love's sexuality re-connects us with our animal roots

Our bodies are what make us human. They are also what make us animals. Our sexual instincts prove we are mammals, yet we tend to forget that sexual love involves two animals as well as two persons. The difficulty is that while love's sexuality requires the release of our anarchic animal instincts, human culture depends upon their repression and control. This dilemma is at the very heart of our human predicament. The forces of nature that keep our species alive – our instincts – are in opposition to the forces of society that make us human – our conditioning. To create peaceful ordered societies, we have made laws that inhibit the free expression of our instincts, and have traded our natural spontaneity for the comforts of civilisation. To live together in human communities, we have alienated ourselves from the community of other animals. This distance from our own animal nature and other animals gives us power over them, as well as language, self-control and abstract thought, which has enabled us to build cities, roads, pyramids and space ships. But all these have come at a price.

We have cut ourselves off from the mystical connection to all life that informed and nourished our ancestors. We no longer enjoy the natural instinctive bliss of the animal, where impulse and action are one. We have numbed the feeling in our bodies. We have lost respect for the animal, and in doing so have lost respect for life.

The greatest gift and greatest curse of our species has been this collective betrayal of our animal nature. Yet we can be human only to the degree we can be animal. We can be alive only so long as we care for the animal body. Any species that neglects its animal body soon becomes extinct. When we repress and deny our animal aspects, we diminish our natural sexuality, limit our capacity to make love and ultimately threaten our continued existence on this planet.

The secret of a happy love life is to care for each other's animal needs

Sexual love brings us back into the reality of our animal bodies, the root of our aliveness. When we fall in love, the sexuality of our love re-awakens the animal instincts and the beast returns. The love made through sexual love, therefore, has the potential to redeem this tragic betrayal of the body. We meet ourselves and our partners as animals, not only as persons. But for reasons I've mentioned, this is not always easy.

My partner and I have a cat. Every morning the cat comes up to our bedroom, onto the bed and has a drink of water out of a particular saucer. When we offer him water in a different saucer he leaps off the bed and leaves us in disgust, tail vibrating in protest. One morning I laughed at him, saying how silly he had become in his old age. Later that day my partner brought me a cup of tea, but in the wrong cup. I told him that surely he knew I only drank this particular tea from that particular cup, and that it didn't taste the same otherwise. This time *he* laughed. But he got me the cup I wanted. He knows that if he doesn't take care of the irrational in me, I will become unhappy without being able to explain why. Were he to challenge me, demanding that I explain exactly why I wanted this cup and this cup only, I might be stuck for an answer. Any reason I would produce could be demolished by scientific logic. My mind might be challenged, even stimulated, but the animal that I am would be hurt and retreat. And when the animal in us retreats, so does the sexual expression of our love.

In this culture, we tend to place a lot of emphasis upon other aspects of relationship, such as shared interests, talking about things and understanding each other. However, in my experience, the secret of a happy marriage lies more in the natural bonding between two happy animals, the instinctual love of the body, than in any meeting of minds. When the animal aspects of ourselves and our partners are cared for, our bodies are happy and we make love naturally and spontaneously. As a consequence, a strong energy field of love evolves, and it is this, rather than what we do, that keeps us in love with each other. Living in the energy field of love is being in love. Taking care of each other as animals and responding to what the animal needs, is therefore of vital importance.

The practical details of daily life are key matters for our animal needs

All social animals have various rituals to greet each other. We need them. The way we greet each other and say goodbye is very important, but not in ways that can easily be explained logically. Experiment with paying special attention to how you meet and leave each other. Notice how different ways of saying hello and goodbye feel. Contrast this with the times you are casual or pay no attention to this.

The general atmosphere of the home is also very important for our animal aspects. Is it warm and welcoming. Is it peaceful and safe? Can you easily rest and relax in it? Walk around your home together as animals, and notice how your body responds to different rooms, colours and the arrangement of furniture. If you did not feel good with anything as an animal, change it, however stylish it may be. Feng Shui is really about encouraging an energy flow through a home in ways that support our natures, and this is not an abstract disembodied 'spiritual' thing – it is about attuning to our natural animal needs.

Pay attention to what animals enjoy, and consciously bring those things into your life. Stroke and touch each other whenever you feel like it, talk nonsense, go for walks, take care of the food you eat, make sure your bed is comfortable, attend to each other's physical needs and creature comforts. Don't, for example, throw out your partner's favourite chair because it doesn't fit with the decor.

Allow yourself and your partner to change your minds for no apparent reason. Let yourselves have irrational feelings about people and situations without trying to change them or be sensible.

Develop routines and rituals that give you pleasure and security, as well as having fun, excitement and adventure. They do not have to make much sense. For example, you may have a special spoon for your cereal, a favourite cup for your tea, or a symbolic ritual at bedtime that has meaning only for you. And respect the routines of your partner, however meaningless, illogical and irrational they appear to you.

Pay attention when either of you have pain or are not feeling well. Don't brush such things aside, however small. When your partner is ill, ask whether they want to be left alone, to be read to, to have music or a video put on, or to be quiet in a darkened room. Ask them what food would they like, whether they want the windows open or closed, or extra blankets on the bed. Likewise, when you're ill, have your partner care for you in the same way. All these practical considerations mean a lot when we are not well.

Ask yourself and your partner *what* you feel, more than *why* you feel that way. Do not expect either of you always, or even most of the time, to be able to explain yourselves to each other. Accept that the only reply to 'Why did you do it?' may sometimes be only 'Because I did'. Explanations, justifications and analyses are not really relevant to animals. Ask a cow why it eats grass and it will simply continue chewing. Ask a cat why it scratches and it is likely to yawn and lick itself. Ask your partner why they did something (and, let's face it, we usually do this only when we don't like what they've done), and they may try to explain, but what they might really want to do is carry on chewing or yawn.

To understand our animal aspects, we must pay attention to our bodies

If you find your sexual love is fading, it may be because you have been neglecting the animal needs of yourself and your partner. This happens easily as our culture and education pay far more attention to the needs of the intellectual mind than the needs of the animal body. Growing up for most of us meant putting aside our more animal desires so that we could learn to think, calculate and read. It is hard to reverse this in our intimate sexual relationships. Not only that, but when our animal needs are not being met, it is hard to articulate exactly what is wrong. It is usually felt as a vague unhappiness, that something is not quite right but we don't know what, that we feel irritated, bored or unhappy for no apparent reason. Discussing the problem will rarely get to the root of what is needed. Ask a dog what it needs and it may bark or wag its tail, but it will not tell us. Our animal needs also do not use verbal language to communicate.

The only way to find out what an animal needs is to observe them, learn the language of their behaviour and interpret what we notice through our own instincts. So when our partners frown and say things we know are untrue, or weep without making any sense, or break agreements, or refuse to do what we think they should, we may need to find a different way to understand them than trying to get them to talk. We need to learn how to understand what their animal aspects are trying to communicate, and this will not be through words.

In the eyes of animals can be seen the soul of the Earth

The word 'dumb' has come to mean stupid, but what cannot be spoken is often a deeper wisdom than any analysis. Reality itself can never be put into words anyway. Communities all over the world use silence to honour victims of tragedies. When there is nothing that can be said or done, silence is the ultimate statement. So when faced with the inarticulate speech of the heart, the language of the unspoken and unspeakable, we may be asked to encounter more profound realities than we realise. And when confronted with the deepest truths of all, there is always nothing to say. We are struck dumb with awe and wonder.

I was on safari in Kenya, when a large giraffe, with intelligent curiosity and the dignity of her freedom, bent down and peered into our jeep. For what seemed like an age we gazed at each other. In her brown eyes I became aware of a vast emptiness, and though 'no-one' was there, I sensed a profound and powerful presence. Looking into the eyes of an unafraid wild animal, we see directly into the soul of the Earth. This is what the antelope sees in the eyes of the lion that kills it, and what the lion sees in the eyes of its prey. It is what we see in the eyes of old people who are not afraid of death. And this is what lovers see, gazing into each other's eyes while making love.

We are also wild and beautiful animals, especially when making love. And through the animal we are closest to, our own body, we understand that sex, love and death are not abstract ideas but carnal mysteries. Sexual love opens up for us the secret wisdom of Earth – that the animal is sacred, that the soul is the body, that incarnation not transcendence is what it's all about. But these truths are revealed only to those brave or fortunate enough to know deep sexual love.

We control the way life flows through our body as a way to control our experience. Sexual love challenges this

The body is both a map of our experience and the source of that experience. Everything that has ever happened to us has left its trace in some form or other in our bodies. The chronic patterns of tension in our muscles, the functioning of our glands and hormones, the wear and tear in our organs and skeletal structure, and the neural networks and electricity of our nervous systems have all been affected in some way by everything we have experienced. When we talk about a feeling, motivation, desire or conflict being unconscious, we mean it lives in our body, in our energy, but not in ways we consciously know about. The body *is* the unconscious. The unconscious is not an abstract concept invented by Freud with no material existence – it is a living entity, the body. Sexual love, therefore, works on many levels that we know nothing about with our conscious minds. Yet our instincts, the life force and energy of our bodies, are directly connected with these hidden dimensions. In sexual intimacy, love works through these instincts.

One aspect of our unconscious life is the way our digestion, blood circulation, brain function and such like all continue keeping us alive in a dynamic homeostasis, subtly balancing themselves, without our being consciously aware of the complex processes involved. We do not have to consciously decide to increase our secretion of bile by the liver, to counterbalance the pancreatic absorption of sugar, to align with the metabolic rate determined by the thyroid to balance the . . . and so on. Life happens. Our instincts take care of it all.

Another aspect of our unconscious life is that we are able to control what we feel and experience by tensing our muscles. The tension takes our attention away from the original sensations and therefore minimises what we feel. We also tense our muscles to inhibit and control spontaneous movement, to prevent ourselves doing things we learned would lead to pain. For example, we stop ourselves reaching out if no-one responds, or keep quiet when we know that making a fuss will cause trouble. In different ways we have all learned to control our bodies as a way to control our experience and what happens to us.

These control patterns eventually become so habitual and structured into the way we breathe, move and hold ourselves, that we no longer feel anything. We also forget what it was that originally caused us to shrink from our experience, or prevent ourselves reacting spontaneously. Like the Indian sadhus who hold an arm above their heads and eventually cannot feel it, move it or even notice it, we no longer feel or notice these tensions. The body has become habituated to them and numb, and we can no longer voluntarily relax or move these muscles even if we wanted to. Our hunched shoulders, contracted bellies, shallow breathing, tight jaws, collapsed chests, puffed-up chests, stiff legs, tight pelvises, tense buttocks, or whatever is our unique combination of chronic muscular tension, are all testaments to the painful and difficult struggles of our lives so far. If our natural life force is weak, or our life has been particularly difficult, our history will be more marked in our muscular structure than otherwise. But all of us have this to some degree.

When we make love as adults, the flow of sexual energy and feeling is inhibited to the same degree that we have this deep tension in our bodies. Reich described this deep muscular tension as a form of body armour that protects us from being hurt, but which undermines our vitality, health and capacity for love. Sexual love dissolves some of this tension, freeing us up so that we can feel, live and love more deeply. This means feeling everything more intensely – both pleasure and pain – and there are parts of us that resist this opening just as there are parts that long for it. This conflict also has a psychological dimension.

Our personality is only the superficial veneer of who we really are – our bodies hold the full reality

The conscious ego, the personality, is the psychic counterpart of the tension in our bodies. If we have stopped ourselves reaching out to others because no-one responded, then eventually we begin to think of ourselves as someone who is self-sufficient, who doesn't need others. If we have forced ourselves to smile and sing under all difficulties, then we will eventually think we are a cheerful person who is never depressed. So as we let go into the sexual energies of the body we are not only helping to relax the deep tension in our bodies, we are also dissolving the inhibitions and restrictions our ego places on our energy. Self-sufficient personalities need their needs and dependencies to become whole, just as cheerful people need their sadness and distress to become complete. As our energy begins to flow we realise that our personality, who we thought was us, is in fact only a relatively small part of who we are. Sexual love allows us to discover how alive we really are, beyond the confines of our personality. For example:

> *A man had learned not to feel how much he needed things from others. He came across as a strong, silent type, a loner, who had much to give, but who did not himself need much. He met a woman who had learned to please those around her. She came across as vulnerable and pliant, easy-going and fun to be with. As is the way of things, they fell in love. She loved the way his strong arms held her.*

He loved the way she leaned appreciatively on him. Then the day came when his strength began to feel like domination and control, and her leaning on him seemed demanding and draining. They began to fight. But not all the time.

They continued to make love. The playful intimacy of the woman and her expressions of appreciation began to melt the tough hardness in the man's chest. He began to feel his heart, his vulnerability and his need. He also began to feel his unfulfilled longing and sadness for the first time. The loyalty and strength of the man began to relax the woman's fear and insecurity. She became more confident and more assertive. She began to feel her passion and desires. She also began to feel her anger and rage for the first time. For a period it was tough between them as the false strength in the man melted away and the phony pleasing behaviour of the woman stopped. In their place came what had been buried, his need and her aggression. They wondered why on earth they were together. But their love knew. His increased tenderness gave the woman even more confidence, while her increased assertiveness made her more present and allowed the man to feel his need for her all the more.

They continued to make love. The man continued to soften, and the woman's confidence in the relationship grew. Eventually the man's true strength broke through, the strength that had enabled him to develop his independence and self-reliance in the first place. But this time it was connected with his need and vulnerability, not alienated from them. The woman's true capacity for love also came through, the love that had allowed her to develop her capacity to care for others in the first place. But this time it was connected with what she needed as well, not only with what others wanted.

There is often a period, when the body armour begins to dissolve and melt under the heat and energy of sexual and emotional intimacy, when the two people no longer feel in love with each other yet it still feels right to be together. Often at this point they will realise that each is not the partner of their dreams but a real-life person who will never be the perfect mate (except, of course, that the perfect mate is never a dream, always a reality). This period can be very confusing as we also realise we are not who we thought we were either. The struggle to find the authentic self, however, is one we all encounter, as losing parts of ourselves seems to be an inevitable consequence of

Dealing with fear is basically very simple. You stop what you are doing and be still. This releases you from being driven into action by your fears and ultimately creating more situations to be afraid in. Once still, you feel your underlying fear rather than running from it. You then face your fears directly. You may find there are things that need dealing with, such as unresolved hurts, neglected needs, forgotten memories, or false beliefs. But once you have stared your fears in the face, you will always find that they have no more power over you. The power of our fears cannot withstand our direct gaze. Their power lies only in telling us to run from them.

We all have deep fears whatever we might think

When we live in fear we cannot live in love, just as when we live in love, though fear may be in us and at times needs to be, we no longer live in fear. This is why love, working always to create more love, will bring to the surface many fears and anxieties. Sexual love, more than any other love, will do this because it involves the deep fears buried in our bodies, long lost to our conscious minds, but which nevertheless affect our behaviour and the way we relate to others.

Surrendering to the pleasures of sexual love is liberating and delightful, but the deeper we go into the pleasures, the deeper are the feelings that emerge. We become afraid of the feelings themselves, and afraid that their intensity will overwhelm the conscious ego we have so painstakingly constructed to keep such threatening feelings at bay. We fear that the deep feelings being released will drown, disintegrate and annihilate us. If we are identified more with our feelings, this tends to be experienced as a fear of death. If we are more identified with our thoughts, this tends to be experienced as a fear of madness. We all have these fears to some extent, and sexual love will usually, at some point, bring us face to face with them. This is partly because, until we face our fears and realise we are stronger than they are, we will be controlled by them, and this leads to neither freedom nor love, and love will always work to make us free to love.

Our fear of death and madness are really aspects of our fear of life

Fear of death is really fear of the unknown. Fear of the unknown is really some projected fear from what has already happened. We can only be afraid of something that has, in some form or other, already hurt us. A burned child dreads fire, while the rest are curious, cautious and fascinated. What we are really afraid of is not what may happen in the future, but what has already happened in the past. By feeling the reality of that old hurt, together with the present fear, we bring life back to the parts we had deadened. By coming back to life through feeling the realities lying in ou

developing thought and language, just as feeding them again creates awareness and self-consciousness.

Sexual love shows us the nature of true integrity

Animals live with unconscious integrity. Human beings have to lose this integrity, this wholeness, in order to find it again and live with conscious integrity.

Living by principles involves, in the first place, dissolving the power of the instincts and fragmenting the first integrity of the animal body. These principles are initially given to us from outside authorities, such as our parents, teachers and society. This always involves some form of violation to the simple spontaneity of the young child. One of the deepest sufferings in being a parent is that you have to interfere with the innocent simplicity of your children, yet there is no other way to become human. Later in life we have to discover for ourselves our own true integrity.

True integrity involves evolving principles that no longer violate the unconscious integrity of the body. Sexual love helps us re-integrate our fragmented selfhood to include the instincts of the animal and the spontaneity of the body, as well as the principled commitment to doing what is right. No amount of teaching through words, ideas and intellectual understanding can lead to true integrity. The learning has to include the wisdom of the body and the instincts of the animal, and there is no better teacher for this than an intimate sexual relationship. We cannot avoid the realities of the body in sexual love. The physical intimacy will confront us repeatedly with the passions and drives of our instincts, and the absolute reality of the sensations of the body. Any ideas or principles that violate this will be challenged repeatedly, either in the form of conflict with our partners or the loss of the sexual expression of our love.

The ego develops through control over the body. To come alive involves surrendering that control. To be always and everywhere in control of our feelings and self-expression makes us tense, anxious and not able to freely move, which is why so many psycho-spiritual processes talk about the death of the ego. We need both the ability to contain and control ourselves *and* the capacity to let go and surrender, to follow our principles *and* our instincts.

The most intimate surrender of all is to our body. Sexual love teaches us to allow our spontaneous involuntary movements again, to let go into the body and surrender to our feelings and sensations. Our sexuality intrinsically involves a surrender to the body, and therefore can re-integrate our selfhood with our instincts and show us how to evolve principles that affirm rather than deny the life of the body, principles that honour life and do not violate it.

The true integrity that affirms life, that includes the instincts of the body as well as the principles of our awareness, is the ultimate authority to which we are answerable, the only true arbiter of what is right and wrong. Rules and ideas of duty and morality can never incorporate the spontaneous anarchic instincts of the animal body. And only when our mind, body and spirit are fully integrated, can we be whole, integrated and no longer divided from ourselves and life.

Sexual love re-integrates us with ourselves, each other and all life. This holy wholeness makes everything sacred. Our collective betrayal of the body is healed. Our inner fragmentation made whole. Our natural instinctual bliss returns and we belong again to the community of all animals.

The sacred animal is the body. By giving the life and love that belongs to the body to an artificially created idea of a soul, we reduce our beautiful animal body to a machine. The organism becomes a mechanism to be used as an object in the service of our minds. The truth is our minds should be serving the wisdom of the body. We have it the wrong way around. Incarnation not transcendence is what it is all about. The body does not ascend to the spirit – the spirit arrives in the body.

CHAPTER THIRTEEN

From Fear to Freedom

In the spreading union of lovers and beloved
this is the true religion. All others
are thrown away bandages beside it.
RUMI

When we live in fear we cannot live in love

Sexual love is a powerful process. It frees our bodies from their chronic tension, our hearts from their fears, and our minds from their restricted ideas of what is possible for us. And it also makes us fall deeper into love. We become aware that we are capable of far more feeling than we thought possible – more love and more anger, more need and more ruthlessness, more desire and more rage, and more sexuality. We might find ourselves in tears, enraged, deeply confused, lonely or overwhelmed with sexual feeling – sensations that are unfamiliar to us can suddenly well up inside us. But this is what happens when love enters our lives, and even more so when this love begins to work on and through our bodies in sex.

What opposes love is not hatred or anger, but fear. Fear contracts us away from life, whereas love takes us into a deeper engagement with life. Fear petrifies us, turning us to stone, while love helps us flow with our energy. Fear makes us try to control life, while love allows us to let go into life. When we live in fear, our world progressively shrinks, but when we live in love, our world continuously expands. This is why, when we fall deeply in love, after a while we also become afraid. Every step into love involves a corresponding step through fear.

We may become afraid that our partner will die or leave us, that they will use our vulnerability to have power over us, or that our love will bind us to them in ways that imprison us. There are many fears in all of us, and sexual love will bring these to the surface more than any other kind of love. These fears unknown, even to ourselves until they surface, are what drive us to fight so hard at times with the one we love. Driven by our unconscious fears, and until we face them directly, we will fight whenever we are afraid. Sexual love helps here in two ways. It first brings to the surface our buried fears, then offers the safety we need to deal with them through our being physically held and loved by our partners. Feeling our fear in the arms of someone we love and who loves us is easier than when on our own.

bodies, we are no longer afraid of death. We have experienced the resurrection of the body directly through our own return to life. We retain a natural animal fear of death (without which we would be defenceless and easy prey), but we no longer live in fear of death. The fear lives in us, and this makes a world of difference.

We will not strive to stay alive whatever it costs, because some things are worth dying for. What does it profit us to stay alive if we lose all self-respect, freedom, dignity and love? If we have never come fully alive, we will sacrifice even these in order to remain half alive a little longer. But you cannot be alive with a dead body. It is always those who have never loved life enough that fear death the most. When making love we surrender control, dissolve the boundaries of the self, and let go into the unconscious forces of the instincts. These are all forms of death to the ego, to the separate self. The French call orgasm 'le petit mort', the little death. Sexual love shows us that death is in life, not at the end of it. It teaches us not to live in fear of death, and it brings us back to life slowly but surely. We fall in love with life itself as well as more deeply with our partners.

Fear of madness is really the fear that comes from being ungrounded and uprooted from the reality of the body. When we live in our own bodies, inhabiting our own skin, we feel safe and held. When we lose touch with our bodies, we become disconnected from what is real and existentially insecure. The word 'madness' is derived from a word meaning 'change', while 'insanity' comes from a word meaning 'unhealthy' – there's a world of difference between the two. What we call madness is simply the raw chaos of constantly changing life beyond the ordered constructions of the mind. It is the denial of these realities that is the real insanity. To lose touch with the life of the body is to go insane, while thinking that what is alive is mad. To become sane involves a journey back through what can look like madness – that is, the raw energy of the life in our bodies, the pain and suffering that we have buried there, and the spontaneity of the instincts. But if we fear coming alive as if it were madness, we end up insane. The turbulent chaos of life, the instinctual anarchy of the body, and the unpredictable spontaneity of our sexual energy all look like madness when we are afraid of life.

Both fear of death and fear of madness are really different forms of the same fear – fear of life. Sexual love faces us with our fear of both death and madness – the death of the separate ego and the raw chaos of real life beyond the mind – because it brings us face to face with real life, the life of the body. It is only when we are no longer afraid of death and madness that we are no longer afraid of life. And it is only when we are no longer afraid of life that we are no longer afraid of love. Sexual love teaches us not to fear death and 'madness', but to embrace them, and in doing so we learn to love life. This makes us even more available for love. As always, life works to create more life, and love works to create more love. The deep pleasure of sexual love and intimacy is how love persuades us back into life even when we are afraid of it.

Sexual love reveals the sacredness of the animal and the sexuality of the spirit

To fall in love is to invite extremely powerful forces into the heart of our lives. When we allow these forces to work on us through the sexuality of our love, we go beyond the frontiers of our minds and experience profound truths about life and love. Making love takes us through our fears into a deeper capacity for love – real love, embodied love. It teaches our bodies how to love. We become free to feel everything – love, fear, anger, joy and so on. We become free to live and love and laugh. We go into the dark interior energies of the body, the unconscious, where we discover the beauty of the beast and are reacquainted with our animal heritage. We are reminded that all life is sacred, and that the soul of the Earth lies within the animal body. We find that the body is the source of the spirit, not the other way around. And we make love.

This is why I think sexual love in committed intimate partnership carries some of the most profound spiritual teachings available to our modern individualist culture. Nothing else reaches so intimately and deeply into our beings and is so ruthless and powerful in its teachings. I have studied a wide range of psycho-spiritual teachings, from Jungian psychotherapy to neo-Reichian bioenergetics, from Rebirthing to encounter groups, and from psychosynthesis to Primal. I have done Zen, Tibetan, Taoist, Tantric, Sufi and many other forms of meditation. I have been involved in political action and feminism, and, on the other pole, surrendered at the feet of an enlightened Tantric Master. I have lived in communes, been entrusted with a totem by an Australian aborigine, danced all night, astral-travelled, run with wolves and channelled the wisdom of higher beings. I have also done housework, brought up a child, worked as a waitress, cleaner, clinical psychologist, cocktail shaker, shop assistant, taxi driver, psychotherapist, factory worker, lecturer and cook, and travelled all over the world. But nothing has touched me to the same depths and intensity as my sexual relationship with my partner and our love. Our journey of more than 20 years together, including two apart, has taught us more than anything else we have experienced. But it was a long time before we realised we had the most powerful process of all in our own back yards – or even closer, in our bed.

Our bodies know the power and depth of sexual love even when our minds do not, which is why so many films, songs, poetry and dramas are about the mysteries and depths of the human heart and its longing for love. Our bodies know we are from love and of love, are born to love and *are* love.

Jung wrote that the spirit is the living body seen from within, and that the body is an outer manifestation of the living spirit – the two being really one. He also said that he did not believe in God – he *knew* God. Lovers know God, too. They know that everything is holy, that no place, person, time or thing is more special than any other, that it is all here, all the time and everywhere. The sexuality of love reveals the ultimate authority of the body. Sexual love reveals its divinity.

Love's sexuality shows that God lives not in heaven, but in our bodies and in everything that moves and breathes. As Eastern spiritual masters have told us long ago – 'This very body, the Buddha; this very Earth, the lotus paradise.'

CHAPTER FOURTEEN

How to Make Love So You Make More Love

Love sits beside me like a private supply of itself.
Love puts away the instruments,
and takes off the silk robes. Our nakedness
together changes me completely.
RUMI

It is hard to talk about our experiences of sex, not only because the instinctual energies of sexuality are difficult to express in words, but because sex itself is a very private affair. No-one knows how two people make love, other than the people themselves. This is completely natural and how it should be. On the other hand, we also need information, knowledge and the wisdom of others. The difficulty is that when we listen to the advice of others, however expert, what they are telling us may not be what is right for us. And although it helps to learn as much as we can from others, ultimately we must rely on our own experience, especially in areas as intimate and private as the way we make love.

If you feel in love with each other while making love, then there is nothing to worry about, whatever position you do it in, for however long, and however many orgasms you have or do not have. Read books, try things out, explore new possibilities if you want to, but simply enjoy yourselves. We only need to pay attention to these things when something is making us unhappy. Unhappy bodies cannot make love. And any unhappiness in a relationship *always* needs engaging with, whatever its source.

One of the first steps to a happy love life, and in order to find our own way of making love, is to put aside most of what others have told us should or should not be happening. Just as each relationship is unique and different, so are the ways we make love. After the First World War many soldiers had apparently lost sexual feeling because of injury to or loss of their sexual organs. Later, however, it came to light that many of the happily married soldiers who were affected were able to have a different kind of sexual feeling spread through their bodies. Some also experienced a peak of pleasure, similar to an orgasm, but again through a different part of their body. One man felt his 'orgasm' through his legs, another through a feeling of love that welled up and took him over. Just as the homeostasis of the body will organise for other organs to take over as much as possible the function of a damaged or diseased one, so too will other parts of the body take over feeling sexual if injury or disease affects the sexual organs. Sexual feeling itself has many aspects, not only sexual behaviour.

The more our life energy flows freely through our bodies, the more we feel sexual throughout our body anyway. Wilhelm Reich discovered that when all emotional holding in the muscular armour of the body is relaxed, then life flows through the whole body without inhibition. Reich said that when making love, this complete surrender to pleasure leads to a total orgasm involving every cell in the body. I and many others in the '60s and '70s sweated and struggled through hours and hours of painful bio-energetic exercises, a form of torture really, where we would bend backwards over stools while therapists beat parts of our bodies with fists or pushed knuckles into any tense areas. The screams were allegedly essential to the full liberation of our energy. Even now, when we meet comrades from that time, we recount to each other old war stories of the pains we suffered in the pursuit of sexual liberation and the ultimate orgasm.

All this bodywork certainly opened up our bodies, deepened our breathing, released chronic tension in our muscles, and brought more feeling and life to our bodies, and we were definitely more healthy and energetic than before. This, of course, led to deeper and more pleasurable experiences during sex. But it also gave us the idea that unless we had a great orgasm, a simultaneous one, a multiple one, a vaginal one, a clitoral one, a prolonged valley one, an earth-moving one, or whatever, then we must be doing something wrong. We forgot that just as the search for the perfect relationship leads *away* from the real relationship, where we *will* find what we're longing for, then searching for the total orgasm takes us away from enjoying making love.

The night before I got married to my first husband when I was 21, my mother took me aside and told me: 'It's like cooking you know, you get better with practice'. I said 'Thanks Mum' and we went back to making the sandwiches. Unknown to her, I had already had sexual experiences she could not even imagine. Yet, in many ways, she was right. The point of cooking is to make eating pleasurable and nourishing, just as sex education should help make sex pleasurable and nourishing. There are some who are gourmets, become innovative cooks and create amazing dishes with new combinations of flavours. These can then offer tips to the rest of us so that our more ordinary fare becomes a bit more spicy. And this is all good. But basically, the sex that is right for us is the sex that gives us the feeling of being in love. Simple really, but then simple things tend to become complex in our complicated minds.

This chapter is not about how to have amazing orgasms or sex for 10 hours. It is about how to create the conditions for your own way of making love to emerge. So, once again, the first step is to appreciate the unique way you enjoy making love. When you sit comfortably in your own sexuality and love-making, you can explore whatever you wish, and it will not take you away from what is most important, which is making love. And this is not always the same as having amazing orgasms. And, anyway, even orgasms, as we have seen, can be very different experiences for different people.

> *A couple came to couple's counselling. The woman said she was unable to have an orgasm and felt she must be frigid. She was wondering if perhaps she had been sexually abused as a child, though she had no conscious memory of this. Her partner was doing everything he knew to help her have an orgasm. They had been doing bodywork, primal therapy, Tantric workshops and all sorts to help her, but nothing changed. She felt ashamed and a failure as a woman, and he was beginning to feel inadequate and a failure as a man. Their life together had become dominated by this issue, and both felt a tremendous pressure that she should have an orgasm when making love. It had all become very serious.*

Now there may well have been issues for both of them buried in their childhoods – feelings of failure and shame, chronic bodily tension, fears and inhibitions – and they could spend their time exploring these, through various therapies, which would certainly help them. But there is another way. The body of their love can be nurtured into a stronger energy field that can then guide them through their difficulties. This was a paradox – for them to make love, they needed to make more love.

> *I suggested they first shift their focus away from what was wrong and onto the ways in which they felt 'in love'. To begin with, they talked about their emotional intimacy and doing things together. Their homework was to actively engage in these. Gradually they felt more emotionally connected with the body of their love. The next step was to find ways in which they felt physically close and loving towards each other. This included cuddling-up on the sofa to watch videos, dancing together, eating out and walking home arm in arm. They made time to focus on these physical intimacies until they could*

consciously begin to feel their love for each other in their bodies. The
next step was to let this love in the body express itself sexually.

This is a different way to approach sexual feeling – not directly but through the feelings of love. But really, sexual energy and love in the body are identical, just described differently. This approach is especially useful when one or other partner has lost sexual feeling. One way to encounter your sexuality through your love is to sit side by side, facing the body of your love, attuning to and feeling your love in your bodies. Then turn and face each other, continuing to feel your love. To feel your love in the first place may take some time and require the release of whatever may be in the way. This involves each sharing with the body of the relationship any worries, resentments, hurts, etc, as described in previous chapters. For some, this energy, this love in the body, is felt first as sexual and later as love. For others, this energy is felt first as love and later as sexual.

This couple discovered that when they explored their sexuality
through their love, the woman had no difficulty experiencing an
orgasm, but it was an orgasm she felt in her heart, not her genitals.
She described it as an explosion of joy that took her breath and mind
away. As soon as she and her partner realised this was her way of
enjoying their love-making, the trauma and heaviness disappeared.
She felt released from many years of feeling something was wrong
with her, and the man felt relieved from feeling burdened with the
responsibility for her sexual fulfillment. And who knows what might
happen as a result of this release and new-found lightness? But then,
that is not for us to know. Just for them to enjoy.

So, first having put aside some of your ideas of what sex and making love should be, and learned to appreciate your own unique way of making love, we can now look at some general types of sexual difficulties.

There are two ways to avoid the vulnerability and totality of sexual love – to go over it or under it. Most sexual difficulties in a relationship fall into one of these categories – oversexualisation or undersexualisation. The first places too much emphasis on sex, while the other avoids and does not engage with sex. Both are ways to avoid the deep vulnerability involved in making love.

If we place too much emphasis on sex, sex often becomes like a drug, a way to sidestep uncomfortable realities and avoid what else may be going on in the relationship. Rather than engaging with issues directly, we distract ourselves and our partners by having sex. This undermines intimacy as it basically avoids dealing with difficult issues between you. It also can lead to a sexualisation of our life. We might behave inappropriately sexually at work. We might sexualise friendships. We might neglect more mundane aspects of life. We might bring a sexual charge to relationships that have nothing to do with intimacy and end up destroying them. We might think sex is what life is really about and become messianic about it.

For the persons themselves, this all makes complete sense, and because they feel a sexual charge in many situations they can easily believe they feel things more deeply than others. Oversexualisation of relationships does give an intense high, as intense as those experienced in extreme sports or partying on cocaine, which can easily create the feeling that this is what life is really about. People in this situation do not realise that they might be using sex to avoid more vulnerable meetings with others, or using their sexuality to have more power over people and situations. They tend to see others as repressed and less alive than they are, not aware that it is they who are in fact out of touch with many of their feelings, and that they have substituted feeling sexual for their more uncomfortable feelings of fear, need, disappointment and sadness.

All this makes acknowledging oversexualisation very difficult, and people in this situation are usually in denial about what is really going on. It often happens that only when they are in love with someone who repeatedly confronts them with the destructive consequences of their behaviour that they begin to acknowledge what is happening. And even then, only when the body of their love has greater power than the sexual habit, will this make much difference. It may be only after their partner has left them that they begin to face how they have not been making enough love, though they are likely to have had loads of sex.

Oversexualisation of relationships has many effects on both the person and their relationships. If this is our problem, then we:

- Experience a lot of pressure that sex has to be fantastic, all the time.
- We have to be sexual, charismatic, attractive, and 'on' whenever we are with others. We cannot relax and simply be.
- We keep changing partners when the mundane realities of ordinary life enter the picture after the highly charged and sexual honeymoon.
- We have difficulty being real and honest but think being sexual is being real and honest.
- We sexualise many relationships, which makes it difficult to commit to one sexual partnership.
- The fantasy of perfect sex interferes with enjoying the intimacy of real love-making.
- We cannot build deep and lasting relationships.

Oversexualisation within intimate partnerships feels great to begin with. Sex is so good that you feel carried by the energy into cosmic realms where this is what life is all about. But what is not happening is a level of engagement with the other *person*. Being more real with your partner would lead to irritations, problems, demands, needs, jealousies and insecurities, all of which are not pleasurable. This is why some have called this sex addiction, because we turn to the pleasures and distractions of sex to avoid real life. And, whatever our choice of drug, this will always be destructive to our relationships.

This is not how it feels, however, because you think that by having sex you are dealing with what matters. Often, a person does not realise what has been going on until they are older, not so attractive or as powerful in the sexual arena, and find themselves alone. Women tend to reach this point earlier than men, as at menopause there is then far less possibility to use one's sexual energy as a means to have power. Men, especially if they have status and money, can continue this kind of life, but are no less lonely on another level, as they may have lost their family by then. But whenever you begin to realise what you have been doing, there is the possibility of recovering.

There are programs to help with sexual addiction such as Sex Anonymous and the 12-Step Program. As with most addictive behaviour, first we need to acknowledge we have a problem. This, as we have seen, is not easy. Then we need to turn to a greater force than our own addiction to help us. This will be through a connection with something greater than our own desires and fears, such as God or whatever is our version of the higher power in the universe, the love of our family, our commitment to the truth, our natural intelligence, or the energy field of all the love we have created during our sexual experiences, as not all of them will have been empty or without meaning. And, whatever else it does, oversexualisation does appreciate the importance of the body and its sexuality, even if this has been used to avoid love rather than to make it.

There is another solution to the problem, too, which is to work on these issues *within* a loving relationship, using the love of the relationship as the higher power. I will go into this later in the next chapter.

Undersexualisation is not the same as having sex infrequently. Some people have a weak sexual charge and do not want sex very often, but when they do they enjoy it. This is not a problem. It may not make the earth move, but it makes love. Undersexualisation is more about there being a hindrance to the flow of sexual energy in the relationship, for instance, when something actively blocks the sexual expression of love. This basically happens when we ignore our frustrations and unhappiness and do not deal with sexual dissatisfaction, or when something has hurt us that we have not deal with. Left unattended, sexual unhappiness means less love is made because of the diminished emotional intimacy this leads to. Eventually, with less and less of a vibrant love life, a couple may stay together but in a resigned fashion, with only a superficial intimacy, perhaps with an underground of resentment. This weakens the energy field of their love and they no longer feel 'in love'. Another possibility we explored earlier is for one partner to have an affair. However, this often takes a more subtle form than involving a third person directly.

The more consciously frustrated partner may have fantasies about others, an inner love affair, which takes them away from real intimacy, just as much as an affair would but less obviously. The sexual energy that should be going into making love then goes into the fantasy and not the reality – masturbation, internet sites, porn films, magazines, etc. The other partner, meanwhile, is likely to find some other outlet for their sexuality, not directly sexual. It might be increased emotional intimacy with friends, a dedication to work, devotional religion or a hobby, but it will not be something that deepens intimacy or engages with their partners, rather something that further diminishes it and distances them.

A frustrated or diminished sexuality always reflects some dynamic in the relationship. Sometimes this is connected with an individual's family history, sometimes with what is happening more immediately within the relationship, but these are always connected. The energy that drew us to our sexual partners in the first place is the energy of our sexual instincts, and our energy always includes our history and experiences. The seeds of future difficulties are there from the beginning, and are an essential part of the complex energy matrix that attracts us to each other. Linking exercises of the kind described in previous chapters can help uncover whatever hidden history might be at the root of this difficulty. Sitting side by side, sharing with the body of your love how you each feel about your sexuality and love-making, allows sensations, thoughts, memories and feelings to rise to the surface. By bringing your present love to fears and wounds from the past, you directly heal and release them. After having brought the deeper hidden currents of your sexuality to light, you can use the love of the relationship in a more intimate way by turning to face each other, holding hands and being absolutely honest about what you are thinking, feeling and sensing, without censoring anything. Doing this while naked and lying in each other's arms is a potent way to release old sexual hurts and fears from this and previous relationships and childhood into your love.

It is important for both partners to see such an exploration as being about the relationship, not that one has a problem, is messed up or doing something wrong. Sometimes, a partner who is apparently sexually misbehaving is not only balancing out a hidden dynamic in the relationship, but they may also be keeping the energies of sexuality alive for the relationship, not only for themselves. As Mae West said: 'Being good is nothing to do with it.'

A key aspect of this process is to first ensure you feel the energy field of your love around you, so that even when there is deep fear and shame you feel safe, held and in love. It is easy to run away from painful memories and hurts, but this means running away from your current partner. There is nowhere to run to and nowhere to hide that would be a better place for you to deal with these feelings than your love. To reclaim your lost sexuality from where it has retreated, these old fears need to be released. It is not that you are responsible for healing each other or becoming a therapist for your partner, it is simply that you create the possibility for your love to do it for you.

CHAPTER FIFTEEN

Sexual Healing

Keep looking at the bandaged place.
That's where the light enters you.
And don't believe for one moment
that you are healing yourself.
RUMI

Sexual problems and difficulties can be caused by a wide range of personal issues, many of which can be healed and released using the power of your love. Here are some examples:

- Being hurt as children, leading to a fear of intimacy.
- Absorbing false ideas and attitudes about sexual relationships from others.
- Unreal expectations of what our partners can give us.
- Expecting love to just work for us without needing any effort or particular engagement on our side.
- Being convinced that the way we go about things is the only right way.
- Constantly trying to make our relationship conform to an ideal because that is the only way we think we will get what we need and long for.
- Protecting ourselves from the potential hurts of intimacy by closing down.
- Someone or something matters more to us than our partner.
- We have not sufficiently separated from our parents and so are not free to give ourselves wholeheartedly to another.
- We have so much fear and anxiety that we cannot let go.
- Power plays, ego games, defence mechanisms, body armour, resentments, fears and all the other inevitable consequences of our human ego that divides us from life in order to rule over it.

All of us will have some of these habits and fears, some of the time, to some degree. It is part of our human cultural heritage. If the sexual energy is not strong enough to overcome these inhibitions, or the earlier input was too strong for us, then we will have difficulties enjoying the sexuality of love and will need help. This help might include bodywork, breath therapy, counselling, the 12-Step Program, or whatever form of therapy we are drawn to, as well as dancing, music, art, active sports, walking in nature and eating good food. As soon as we decide to consciously care for our animal bodies in order to nourish our capacity for sexual love, we will discover the best activities and possibilities to meet the deeper needs in our bodies for love.

> A couple had been together for four years. The woman had moved to be in the same city as the man, where they lived together in his flat. They were considering having a baby. They loved each other but the sexuality of their love had diminished. The man was rarely interested in physically making love, and the woman felt rejected and hurt by this.

There may be many reasons behind the man's decreasing interest in physical love-making, and they all need to come to light so that the couple can deal with them. There are also many reasons behind the woman's feeling hurt and rejected, not all of them to do with her partner's lack of sexual interest. Dealing with the man's disinterest in sex through trying to stimulate or excite him will not get to the root of what is happening, and at best will only temporarily solve things. They both need to explore the deeper currents of their relationship to uncover what is going on below the surface. Linking into your love is very helpful here, talking to the body of love of the relationship as if talking to a third wiser body that knows both of you intimately and can be completely trusted to have both of your best interests at heart.

> This couple sat next to each other and looked at their relationship together. They found several things were happening that they had ignored or had not realised were going on. The man was frustrated at work. He played guitar in a band and wanted to spend more time making music and performing. Plus, there were difficulties at work endemic to the organisation he worked for, and therefore not only insoluble but also impossible to address. Yet he could not envisage losing his high salary if they were to soon start a family. The woman, meanwhile, discovered how much she was missing her family and friends since she had moved. She had turned naturally to her partner to meet more of her emotional needs, and although he had understood this, he had experienced it as yet another demand for which he was responsible. He felt burdened and was trying to find the resources within himself to meet these demands, yet in doing so had turned inwards and away from her.
>
> The more they explored, the more the layers underneath revealed

themselves. It emerged, for example, that just as the man had withdrawn sexually, the woman had withdrawn in another way. Because they were living in the man's apartment, she did not feel free to put her energy into the home and had remained distant. The man had felt this lack but had not known how to address it or even what it was.

Having identified some of the key areas causing unhappiness, the next step was to deal with them. Putting up with unhappiness in intimate sexual relationships never works, neither does complaining, suffering in silence, trying to cope alone or pretending everything is fine. All unhappiness must be dealt with.

This man and woman made some key changes to their lives. They pooled their finances, which meant that the money the woman had been keeping separately became available (she had a substantial sum from her parents). This freed the man to work part-time, and he therefore had more time to make music. Her financial support for him was reflected in his increased support for her emotionally, though this happened naturally rather than as a duty. His fulfillment made him less preoccupied and more available. They moved to a flat that was equally the home of them both. The woman's demands for sexual intimacy lessened as her other needs were more in the picture. The man, now flowing with his energy musically, found his energy flowing in other ways, including sexually. They also made sure he shared his burdens more, talking about them on a regular basis, and not keeping them to himself. Likewise, she explored her needs regularly, too, and did not just reach out automatically, expecting her partner to meet them.

Like a log jam that needs just one log moving before it all flows again, the key dynamic that changed everything around was the generosity of the woman in making her money available to support the relationship. Neither of them had realised that in different ways each was keeping vital energies out of the relationship – he, his sexuality, she, her money. The woman simply found she loved this relationship enough to give a significant amount of her money to it, and the rest followed. There was no need for them to engage in explorations of their personal histories or inner worlds. Her generosity was enough for their love to flow again and begin to work once more between them.

Making love is the way our bodies express and experience love

Most sexual difficulties in a relationship arise because something is blocking the flow of love between the couple. Making love involves a surrender into the love in your body, not about doing it a particular way. It is rarely a physical problem. Making love is the way our bodies express and experience love. Anything interfering with the flow of love is therefore likely to show itself in some form of sexual difficulty. It is often easier to deal with sexual issues through the love than through the sexual energy directly, as it is clearer from this perspective that a sexual imbalance or problem is something that involves both. When looking only at sexual behaviour, it is easy to locate the problem within one or other individual which then neglects the relationship dynamics. In the example just mentioned, this could have led to a focus on the man as having a sexual or emotional blockage that should be released, ignoring the other levels of need going on in them both.

Bodies naturally want to make love with each other. What gets in the way are the same kind of dynamics that get in the way of the flow of love on other levels – for example, closed hearts and minds, and the ways in which these affect the flow of love through the body. By creating the space for the love to flow (which in a way is what this whole book is about), we are creating the climate and conditions for sexual love to flow, too. Whether we experience love primarily through the body (sexually), the heart (feelings of love), or through the mind (spiritual connection), this is less important than that we love. The channels through which we give and receive love will be different depending on so many factors in different situations in different relationships.

In intimate sexual partnerships, the love includes *all* levels. Every other kind of relationship is circumscribed in various ways, and there are limits to what can be expressed, expected or communicated. In committed intimate sexual partnerships, it never works to follow a rule book about how to behave, how to assert yourself, how to get what you want, how to be loved, how to express anger creatively, how to negotiate constructively, how to maintain a position, and how to place boundaries. It never works because ultimately the sexuality of love will conform to none of our ideas or attempts to subjugate it. If we try to control the natural expression of our energy with our sexual partners by following a program, then our sexual energy will react, retreat or rebel, which will lead to all sorts of problems. Intimate sexual relationships have at their core our sexual energy and bodies – in other words, our *energy* and not our personalities, egos or practical, managerial, intellectual and organising aspects. Our energy is like nature – it *is* nature, but *this* also means that we must respect it rather than dominate it.

Within sexual love, this is a liberation as well as the source of anarchic confusion. Unlike other kinds of relationship that can only allow a degree of freedom, intimate sexual relationships allow us to be completely ourselves. In fact, they demand this of us. In the heart of our intimate sexual relationships we find the one place on the planet where there are no rules about how to be or what can be expressed. And where we can be most truly ourselves is where we also feel the most love.

> *A woman had been sexually abused by her step-father over a period of years, until she threatened to expose him. She enjoyed sexual relationships with several men until she was married and then suddenly found she could not bear to be touched. Her husband was initially understanding and patient, but naturally became frustrated as time went on. She came to counselling for help as their emotional intimacy as well as their physical intimacy was becoming affected. She was clear they both loved each other and so I suggested that since this was a difficulty they were both experiencing, that they work on it together.*
>
> *They sat together and linked into the body of their love on an empty chair. Immediately the woman felt safer and could open up and share herself with their love-body, but not with her husband. On many levels she was walled off from him. The increased safety of the commitment of marriage had allowed this profound 'no' in her to surface – the 'no' that had once been a great ally and saved her from her abuse. However much the man understood, he was also angry and resentful. They agreed to put aside 30 minutes every day to work on this with their love-body, saying whatever they needed to about anything they wished. They also agreed that whenever things were tense between them, they would not confront each other directly, but communicate through their love-body, which gave the woman a degree of safety she could not feel any other way.*
>
> *Over the next weeks the woman felt safe to express herself freely. She had never felt like this before. She felt less directly exposed and vulnerable, and held by their love, and was able to speak about her sexual abuse for the first time. This brought them very close emotionally, as the man's protective care for her responded to what she was revealing.*
>
> *They continued their Linking daily though the next weeks were difficult. The safer the woman felt, the more her rage began to emerge. The man felt lost and helpless but continued to sit next to her*

because he loved her, even when she was raging about all men. He asked if they could hold hands as he wanted to help her in some way. She angrily rejected him, which hurt him deeply. As she became aware of her anger beneath her protective wall, he became aware of his hurt beneath his anger. What supported them both was their love, and alongside their distress they could also feel their love more and more as a real force in their lives.

The next weeks, persevering with the Linking exercise, saw the man unfolding more and more of his hurt and pain. As he did so, the fierce self-protection of the woman began to melt and she reached out to him. They discovered that he had within him as deep a pain, though very different from hers. He had been sent away to boarding school when he was seven and had been bullied there. He had a well of loneliness and grief inside him that began to come out through his tears.

One day they sat holding hands in front of their love, with little left to say. They simply felt the anguish of both their own and the other's pain. There was a deep meeting, with their love as the witness, with the truth of their painful childhoods. This brought them to a place beyond all their anger and hurt, beyond all their attempts to heal, to forgive, to let go the past, and beyond all their doing. Both of them surrendered to the reality of their deep suffering. They later described this experience as a meeting of their souls and their second marriage. The first had provided the commitment for the deeper realities of their hidden pain to emerge. The second gave them the knowledge that their love could be both the vessel that held them and that carried them through life, as it had already held them through the worst. Even though they knew there were bound to be difficult times still to come, and many more aspects of their childhood pains to deal with, they both felt ready to turn and face each other in the full intimacy of their marriage.

Making love is not something we do – it is what happens when we have created the conditions for love to flow in our bodies

When we surrender into the feelings and sensations of the body, then we will instinctively make love without thinking about it, and our movements will be involuntary, spontaneous and naturally pleasurable. Without consciously doing anything, it will all happen. Ideas of what we should be doing or what ought to be happening will only interfere with this instinctive spontaneity. Yet because we have lost touch with our natural innocence, we often need some help to allow our sexuality its full expression.

So to deal with sexual difficulties through the channel of love involves first creating the space for love to flow. The Linking exercises described throughout the book will help here. There are also specific ways in which we can foster the flow of love through the body, primarily by creating the space for it to happen, as love arrives naturally whenever there is the invitation. Our job becomes to simply create the right conditions for love to flow in our bodies and to then let love do the work. But don't expect deep and complex issues to be resolved overnight. Love more often works like water on a rock rather than in dramatic breakthroughs.

Here are some ways to foster the conditions for love's sexuality to flow.

1   Leave family, friends, therapists, gurus, pets and anyone else outside the bedroom door. They do not belong anywhere near you when you are making love. The only people that should be allowed in your bedroom are your children, and then only when they have a real need for you – unless you are ill or dying, and then your bedroom is a different kind of temple.

2   Do not talk about your sex life with anyone other than your partner except in very broad terms. It is too private and too intimate to be spoken about except to each other. The only time that it is OK is when you are in a protected environment, such as with a therapist, a couple's counsellor or a very trusted friend. And none of these should be a substitute for talking with your partner.

3   Have time together where you are not a parent, colleague, homemaker or any of the other roles you have with each other. Be simply a man and a woman. After all, it is this that brought you together in the first place. The children, the family and the parents are born out of the woman and the man, not the other way around. This usually involves having time away from the family home, where you can be together without these other responsibilities. Love-making happens naturally between a man and a woman who love each other, but not between co-parents, colleagues, accountants, or organisers of the school run, etc.

4   The woman and the man are the primary architects of the family, the twin pillars that hold up the home. Children need and want their parents to be making love because that is the love that feeds and nourishes them. Sexual happiness is an atmosphere in the home that is more helpful for your children than all the educational programs, intellectual discussions and games of football they might also need. By taking time away from your children to nourish your sexual love, you

are actually taking more care of them than were you to be always by their side.

5 Have your bedroom where you are least likely to be overheard – both for arguments and for making love.

6 Use pure cotton or linen sheets on the bed. Nylon and polyester ones create static electricity and the two of you are creating enough electricity for one bed to handle.

7 If your partner doesn't like perfume or aftershave then don't use it. Sex and smell are intimately linked. In sexual love, beauty is in the nose of the beholder, and our natural pheromones are more attractive than chemicals.

8 Find a form of birth control that suits you both and your sexual life style. There's no point using a cap if you have a tendency to make love on mountains, or taking the pill if you are into macrobiotic food.

9 Spend an evening together where you do not talk. One of you is likely to find this easier than the other. You can talk about this later.

10 Have an argument using only animal noises and movements. If you want to scratch or bite or kick then just say 'scratch', 'bite' or 'kick' as you wave your fingernails at your partner, snap your jaws or kick the air. By cutting through the verbals and diving straight into the energy, you often find out what is causing the argument far more quickly.

11 Watch things together – birds, movies, sunsets, art, snakes, sport, museums, or whatever takes your fancy. Side by side, looking at things, fulfills one part of you. Later, turn to each other and use your other senses for a different pleasure.

12 Loosen up the tensions in your body through dancing. Dance along pavements in the rain, in your living room, on your way to work, on the lawn at dawn. Dance to drumming for hours. Dance naked in the dark. Dance slowly, cheek to cheek, hardly moving, and dance with wild abandon and no restraint. Dance the fox-trot and waltz, and dance to hip-hop, soul, rock, or whatever turns you on. Apart from sexual love, dancing is the single most powerful way to release tension and celebrate the life of the body.

13 Swim naked in a warm sea, drink champagne for no reason, fall backwards onto soft clover, breathe clear mountain air, run into rain . . . Let your body and nature have fun together. They are old friends.

14 Once in a while, get drunk together, get stoned, take whatever is your substance of choice to help you over the edge of the known and into the energies beyond the mind.

15 Give each other a massage, cuddle together watching a video, lie in the sun and gossip. Let your bodies enjoy each other in a multitude of ways.

16 Abandon all ideas of how sex should be – romantic, fierce, tender, passionate,

intimate, silent, noisy, planned, spontaneous, quick, slow, familiar, novel, chaotic, controlled, with elaborate foreplay, straight to the point, with the light on, in the dark . . . Let your love-making be any or all of these, as you wish. But let them happen naturally, not when you decide. Do not impose your will onto sex. Sexual love is about a surrender into the deeper love in your body, not about doing it a particular way – except when you want to.

17 Remember that the journey is the goal, not the orgasm.

18 Be honest. If you like something, then let your partner know. If you don't like something, share that, too. You don't necessarily need to actually say anything – your body will communicate it anyway. You only need to speak if the message doesn't reach your partner behaviourally.

19 Sexual love is a microcosm of the relationship. It includes everything, just as the relationship does, from cosmic transcendence to a quickie in the shower. Enjoy the full range.

20 Smell, touch, feel and sound are more important than sight when making love.

21 Remember that you and your partner are different and, although you will enjoy the same things, it is likely you will express your pleasure in different ways. One might make more noise or be more silent. One of you might laugh and cry and feel emotions more, while the other might smile, shake and feel sensations more.

22 Sometimes when you feel sexual, spontaneously make love there and then. Sometimes do nothing but feel it and save it for another time and place. Learning how to hold sexual charge in your body without seeking immediate relief gives you more possibilities to play with.

23 One lies down naked, the other places their hand wherever they want to over any part of the partner's body. Breathe into that part, before moving on to another part. This brings feeling back into parts of your body you may have neglected.

24 Sit or lie facing each other completely naked. One of you focuses on looking and the other simply lets themselves be seen. Then change over. Let whatever is there in you be seen – your fear and shame, your wish to hide, your love, your need, your joy, your vulnerability, your sadness, longing, power . . . whatever is there.

25 Sit facing each other naked, sharing all your feelings, sensations and thoughts.

26 Lie side by side holding hands in stillness and complete silence, with your eyes closed. Afterwards, share any stray thoughts, images, memories or insights that came to you.

27 When making love, say when something feels good.

28 When making love, do not do anything you don't want to. You are there to love yourself as much as another.

29 Lie together and simply feel. Let it all happen, bearing the unbearable nakedness of being in its most intimate form and surrendering to the pleasure.

30 Doing it right or reaching any particular inner state is nothing to do with making love. Being yourself is.

CHAPTER SIXTEEN

The Languages of the Unspoken

They rarely spoke
because of the dangerous seriousness
of the secret they knew.
That love-secret
is a killing better than any living.
RUMI

The energy field of love permeates existence

Love is all around us. As well as the personal loves of intimacy, family and friendship, and the impersonal loves of comradeship, co-workers and fellow travellers, love can enlighten and inform every area of human endeavour, including music, dance, sport, cooking, mathematics, fast cars, astrology, computer games, knitting, collecting shells, and so on. The list is endless. We can love nature, the sea, the mountains, forests, wilderness, other animals, the sun, the stars and life itself. Even what we think of as love's dark counterpoint – hatred, evil, terror, cruelty, abuse – can be transformed through the triumph of the human spirit into love. Witness the achievement of the black people of South Africa – who out of their terrible suffering under apartheid created the Truth and Reconciliation Commission – which has now become a political possibility for the whole world.

In its struggle to turn base metals into gold, love continually tries to reach us through many channels. It reaches us through ourselves, our partners, those around us, our relationships, animals, nature and through simply what happens. The messages can be intellectual, emotional, sensational and spiritual, and interpreted and understood by our minds, hearts, bodies and spirits respectively. That's a lot of different media using a lot of different channels, and love uses them all.

We tend to think of communication as being only verbal, intellectual and emotional exchanges between people, and tend to ignore the dialogues possible with animals, dreams, nature and so on. Verbal language and the spoken or written word work well in scientific papers, business transactions, travel directions and legal contracts, where how to do something is being communicated. But they neglect the parts of us that know more about feeling, sensing, intuition, instinct and being – the parts that are like children, animals and nature. In intimate sexual relationships, these parts are of central importance, and our communications reflect this, even when we may not be aware of it.

Love speaks to us through our child-like aspects

Young children communicate through feelings and emotional expression – for example, crying, smiling and laughing – as well as behaviourally – for example, stroking, running around, refusing to eat, hiding and stealing. Our instincts and feelings give us the meaning of their emotional expressions and behaviour far more than our reason and thought. This is perhaps why we often do not understand what children are trying to tell us. When they lie or steal or bully, we tell them they are wrong and must stop. We may even put them on medication. What we really need to do is try to find out *why they* are doing these things. All behaviour in a child, however disruptive and destructive, has a meaning that is our responsibility to uncover. It is a betrayal of our children to control them without understanding them.

Yet this understanding is difficult, as a child's communication skills are rarely verbal. Though a child may say many things, *what* they say rarely has significant meaning. Play, not conversation, is the primary medium of self-expression for a child, and their emotional and behavioural communications are much more meaningful than their words.

The child in us and the child in our partners also communicate more through what we do and feel than through what we think and say. In intimate sexual relationships, the child in each of us is of supreme importance. The child parts of us hold the keys to intimacy, as without the innocent, unprotected vulnerability of the child there can be no real intimacy.

The self-protection and control we have learned can be put to better use protecting the body of love, rather than, as is usually the case, defending each from the other. The child parts in each can then play together in safety, knowing danger is being kept at bay by other, more powerful parts. Whether we protect and nurture the child parts of the relationship or attack what we perceive is the threat, usually our partner, which further frightens the child, depends upon the balance within the relationship of love and fear. If the fear is dominant, we will attack our partners in some way; if the love is dominant, we will protect and take care of the children within us. It's an old choice – to follow love or fear. The stronger the love-body of the relationship, the easier it is to move through our fears and into love.

A man and woman found themselves repeatedly arguing about all sorts of things, though neither knew why. A chronic unhappiness entered their relationship, which made it even more difficult for them to resolve their fights. One night they both had intense dreams. The man dreamed he was weighed down with armour on a long trek across a harsh landscape, a soldier with no goal in sight and a long way from home. The woman dreamed her cat was lost in a shopping mall, meowing piteously and frightened by all the people rushing around. Both knew these dreams were somehow about their situation together and realised they had to engage with their relationship in a new way. They came to counselling and learned how to tap into their love to help them.

They sat side by side, facing the body of their relationship, and asked their love for help. Immediately they felt less on the defensive. The man took on the role of the soldier in his dream. He spoke as the soldier. He became the soldier. He spoke of his harsh life, the unrelenting way he pushed himself, and the emptiness he felt all around him. This moved the woman, who asked him if he felt any nourishment at all in the bleak landscape. Suddenly he began to cry like a boy, like the boy he had been who had known deep loneliness and sadness as a child. His tears were a deep release and went on for a long time. Now it was the turn of the woman. She took on the role of the lost frightened cat. She felt as the cat did. She became the cat. She felt very afraid and in a panic. She realised she often felt like this, in a state of anxiety that there was danger all around her. The man reached out and held her hand, which made her feel safer. She began to feel her fear rather than escaping it through fighting with him. Eventually she, too, began to weep like a little girl who had been afraid for so long that she had forgotten there was another way to be.

They continued to use their love as a resource, which helped them move through their fight and into the need and vulnerability of the child in them both. This process became a vital part of their life together and brought them very close again. Although they continued to fight at times, as we all do, there was never the same degree of alienation from each other, and slowly these forgotten childlike parts entered the relationship more and more. And with them came many other gifts, both magical and intimate.

Love also speaks to us through our animal aspects

Animals, in their natural instinctive innocence, like children, are closer to some realities than we are. Animals communicate through behaviour – scratching, roaring, running, barking, purring and grooming. When a bull stamps his feet we run, and when a cat rubs against our leg we stroke it. We instinctively respond because our bodies translate and give us the meaning of their behaviour. Most of us, however, turn to our intellectual minds to explain things and have forgotten how to interpret and give meaning to the sensations of our bodies. As a consequence, we generally no longer understand the behavioural communication of animals. Yet both ourselves and our partners are animals. Our sexuality comes from the animal body and has it roots deep in our animal heritage. Deny this, ignoring the fact that we are animals, and the sexuality of our love disappears.

The parts of us that are like other animals are more important than we usually realise and, whatever we think, there has been much wisdom accumulated during the millions of years of evolution. Buddha said that every time a stomach rumbled during meditation, an insight was on its way to consciousness – our reptilian stomachs, it seems, know some things before our mammalian brains.

Communication between our animal bodies are very important. How we move, the way we touch and greet each other, the food we eat and how we eat it, the atmosphere of the home, and the degree of freedom and respect we give to the life of the body are all more important for sexual love than our intellectual discussions or the books we read. A recent survey found that 75% of cat owners felt more loved by their cats than by their partners. Perhaps this is because our pets, in their innocence, love us simply as fellow animals.

Animals themselves can also be love's messengers

Love speaks to us not only through the sensations and instincts of our own animal bodies, but also through animals themselves. They can be messengers of important truths. A friend of ours, a Buddhist, had been wondering whether to take his Bodhisattva vows, which means placing your life in the service of all life. During a meditation he realised he was ready for this, and when he opened his eyes he saw a bird had flown in and was sitting at his feet, blinking up at him. Richard Moss has described how a black butterfly settled on his third eye at the very moment he had a spiritual awakening. Some friends took their son to university and were worried about how he would cope. They saw a dolphin swimming in the nearby sea and their worries lifted. These signs and messages are happening all around us but we have forgotten how to read them, and most of the time do not even notice them.

My partner and I were driving near the Sahara desert at night. I was going over some painful experiences I had been through and describing how I had felt like a terrified, shaking creature caught in on-coming car headlights and how much I had hated it. I suddenly said with a great deal of energy and force: 'I am *never* going to be vulnerable again!' Suddenly, a tiny, fragile, and extremely vulnerable kitten ran out onto the road in front of us and stood shaking, staring into our headlights. A massive overloaded truck was coming very fast towards us on the other side of the road. It seemed this kitten was going to die. But somehow, I don't know how, we managed to swerve, missing both the kitten and the truck. But what was such a tiny kitten doing in the desert of all places?

But I already knew. By rejecting my vulnerability so forcibly I had created a tiny kitten shivering in panic, with nowhere to go. I got the message and took back into myself my vulnerability. There is no way any of us can go through life without being hurt. That poor little kitten had had to go through the terrifying experience of nearly being run over simply because I was not willing to be vulnerable again. However, there must have been something in it for the kitten and catness, too, though what, I will never know.

We have strong minds that limit the realities we can experience.

All of us have many such communications and signs from animals, but we rarely know what they mean or even that they are communications with meaning at all. Civilisations that live closer to the earth than ours know better how to interpret the messages from animals. A visit from an eagle is an invitation to train as a Shaman. A visit from a snake is a sign that you are a healer. The reaction of animals tells you your totem. The movements of lizards and the flights of birds give information about the future. But animals give us information in this culture, too, though with our strong minds we tend to scorn such channels of communication.

Indigenous people describe themselves as having weak minds, and are proud of this. They perceive Western minds as being hard, logical, forceful and difficult to shake from their practical and concrete perceptions. Weak minds do not erect such barriers to an extended reality. They can talk with trees and rocks, dance with the spirits and understand the language of nature and the land. Weak minds can experience realities and life forms that remain hidden to strong minds, and can read the signs from animals and nature more easily than we can. They pity us our strong minds. This is hard for us to understand from the material comfort and security of our modern technology. How could anyone not want the consumer heaven we enjoy, with its freedom from hunger, its material wealth and range of choice? But security and choice are not the same as dignity and freedom.

Wealth and, even more so, freedom can be interpreted in many ways. For some, the freedom to walk across land owned by no-one whenever they wish is worth more than any secure salary and pension with its nine-to-five restrictions and rush-hour hell. And for some, enjoying the sunset outside a log cabin is worth more than owning a Turner painting. Just as diverse as our ideas of freedom are our understandings of love. And our strong minds, so brilliant at keeping us alive and making money, are not necessarily so useful for keeping love alive and making love.

Nature too, speaks to us of love

To comprehend love we need to weaken the hold our strong minds have, not only on the way we think about life, but on the way we perceive and experience life. Reality is not what we think it is. Neither is love. Love is beyond the comprehension of our intellectual minds. It takes us into the forces of nature, into the wisdom of the body and the energies and instincts of life itself. The mind divides matter into its smallest units, analysing and explaining things in terms of the way these interact. Love brings things together to find the meaning, looking for the patterns in the whole.

Nature is a great teacher concerning the holistic designs of love. Nature communicates with us through phenomena, such as storms, droughts, planetary alignments, the movements of insects and birdsong. Again, different civilisations understood this. The year before the Second World War began, the bushmen of the Kalahari were saying a dreadful calamity was about to happen to the whole world. Despite being cut off from all newspapers and media, they knew this simply because of how the birds had begun to sing. Not many listened to them.

Shamans, priests and Jungian psychotherapists translate natural phenomena one way, scientists and politicians another. Comets, earthquakes, floods, migrations have all been given very important meanings throughout human history. In the Middle Ages the birth of a deformed animal was a sure sign of God's fury since it was seen as an abomination of nature, and the priests would read the meaning and what should be done. These days it is a sign of industrial pollution or pharmaceutical abuse and is interpreted by scientists and lawyers.

It is hard for a culture to question its own dogma, and since empirical science is the dominant explanatory paradigm of our society, we rarely challenge its premises. As a result we have forgotten that all meanings are relative, and no longer hear that earthquakes and floods, dying species and genetic deformities may be communications of a different kind. Perhaps they are nature trying to speak to us in a language we no longer understand.

Life is stranger than we think

All life, not only animals, plants and the natural world, can carry important messages and meanings. There are many instances where something has happened apparently miraculously in people's lives – strange synchronicities, inexplicable parallels, uncanny similarities – that cannot be explained by chance alone. This happens not only in dramatic circumstances but is an everyday occurrence, though we do not usually notice it.

A radio programme on synchronicity interviewed at random people on the street. The tenth person questioned happened to be an expert on synchronicity. This man had devoted the previous year of his life to studying synchronicity and reporting his daily findings on his web site. He said the more he looked for strange synchronicities, the more he found. Here was another one. The programme makers, too, found that strange 'chance' events kept happening. Books fell off shelves and landed open at exactly the page describing synchronicities, and people called up just before they were going to be called themselves by the programme makers. I very rarely listen to the radio but in a break while writing this chapter, I 'just happened' to turn on the radio as this programme started. In a further twist, many months later, I again 'happened' to turn on the radio while editing this chapter and this very programme was being repeated!

Just this morning, too, I was speaking with my partner on the phone. He had been through a gruelling experience, the final act of a long story, and was describing how it had ended something that had motivated and driven him all his life. He felt something in him had been destroyed, too, but was not sure if what he was feeling was an emotional reaction of that moment or a deeper truth. He looked up and laughed. A van had just parked in front of him. On the side was printed: 'Absolute destruction guaranteed – www.totaldestruction.com'.

Once you begin looking for these synchronicities and coincidences, as with the patterns of love in relationship, you will find them. Strong minds, however, will find this harder than weak ones.

Love will try to reach us through whatever channel is available

Love, like nature, speaks to us through the phenomena of our lives, through what happens to us. Love communicates through events, circumstances, 'chance' meetings, things that 'just happen', accidents, illness, dreams, nature etc.

Love can also on occasions communicate with us directly from the realms of energy, from the world of the spirit, through a transmission of energy and wisdom into our souls. Dreams, sudden revelations, Satoris, the insights that come to us in meditation or while walking, dawning realisations that arrive quietly, as well as flashes of inspiration and enlightenment – share all of these with your partner.

As a routine every morning, for example, share your dreams. There is no 'right' way to interpret them. Just share whatever responses, pictures, ideas, connections and insights come to you without worrying about whether they make sense or are right.

Love will teach us things we had no idea we needed to learn

Things happen, too, between lovers for no reason that our minds can comprehend. For no reason at all, other than that our love demands we experience them, and in the living of them we come to embody a deeper love. One of the ultimate challenges of human sexual love is to become the embodiment of love itself, to become a body of love – Love's Body on Earth. The phenomenology of intimate relationships may therefore need to be simply experienced with no intellectual understanding possible or even desirable.

But this involves the mind relinquishing its position of control and surrendering to the greater power of experience, the body, which is not easy for most of us. Yet again love comes to the rescue. Sexual love teaches us through pleasure the art of surrendering control and letting go into the energy and experience of the body. While making love you are learning to go beyond the restrictions of the intellectual mind. You can also do this by living in a dark cave, looking at a blank wall for a week, sitting in yoga postures for hours or wearing a hair shirt. But I know which I prefer.

In intimate sexual relationships the adult, the child, the animal, nature and love are all involved, and as a consequence we use five languages with our partners – verbal, emotional, behavioural, phenomenological and spiritual – though we are rarely aware of them all and do not need to be. Generally, the more unconscious the matter to be communicated, then the more behavioural, phenomenological or spiritual is the message. Sometimes we have to leave it to the higher power of our love to sort it all out for us.

A woman and a man loved each other. For years the man tried to tell the woman that her beliefs and ideas of what a good relationship involved interfered with his freedom to be himself. For example, she would withdraw hurt if he did not take care of her in the way she thought he should, or would criticise him if he did not share himself with her emotionally. She had very strong ideas about what loving relationships should involve. She ignored his attempts to communicate with her emotionally and behaviourally, telling him he needed therapy for his fear of intimacy. His expressions of frustration at not being understood – slamming doors, shouting and shaking his fist – were interpreted by her as further proof of his problems in intimacy rather than part of a process between them. This went on for many years. Eventually, he had an affair. This shocked her. Although she was angry and hurt, she also loved this man and her love would not let her simply attack and blame him. She had no other option than to explore more deeply what this was about.

She began to realise that whenever she felt hurt she would turn to him and become angry if he did not stop what he was doing and take care of her. She would do this for him and believed he should do the same for her. But when he was hurt he would always try to deal first with it by himself and would only turn to her when in deep distress. He needed to feel free to help her in his own way and in his time. He didn't want it demanded of him. But as he didn't know why he sometimes felt frustrated with her demands, he could not explain this. Her love helped her see many things.

Fortunately, she began to realise what she had been doing in time and he came back, because he loved her. He had only left because he loved himself, too. And then, of course, it was his turn to learn what he had been doing. He discovered she had been right – he had been afraid of the demands of intimacy and he was afraid of how much he needed her. But now that she respected his freedom, he was able to listen to her. In the reciprocal symmetry of relationship, he turned to her more and she turned to him less. He taught her about freedom and she taught him about intimacy. They found what they had both been longing for – love and freedom, themselves and each other.

CHAPTER SEVENTEEN

The Meaning of Phenomena

Last night we listened to your one story,
of being in love. We lay around you,
stunned like the dead.
RUMI

Love will keep turning up the volume until we listen

For our intimate relationships to be deep, fulfilling and loving, we have to pay attention every time we hurt each other. Accumulated neglected hurts eat into and destroy intimacy. However, we don't feel the ways we hurt our partners – they do. Similarly, we feel the ways they hurt us and they don't. So for us to learn how we hurt our partners, we cannot rely only on our own views and experience. We have to listen to them. The trouble is that when someone is hurt, they rarely speak clearly and directly about it. They tend to attack, disconnect or freak out. Trying to find the hidden meaning of a partner's behaviour may be impossible in the heat of the moment, and sometimes a row is what's needed anyway, and understanding can happen later. Love can work its magic through almost anything between lovers.

If we do not pay attention to our partners when they are hurt, then they will adopt a more behavioural way to communicate, such as shouting, slamming doors, becoming depressed, smashing crockery, and refusing to speak. Love will keep trying to get the message across.

Whenever someone feels their distress has been ignored, they will try other means to communicate. The more resistant we are to hearing what they have to say, the more behavioural or phenomenological will become the ways in which they communicate. This can happen between nations as well as partners. One nation may, for example, resort to violence and suicide missions if their frustration and suffering has been ignored and dismissed by the usual diplomatic and channels of dialogue and communication. Driven by rage and despair, they destroy themselves as well as those who don't listen. This can happen in intimate relationships, too.

Unexpressed feelings build walls between partners

One of the most powerful messages we can give our partners, ourselves and the relationship, is to have an affair. It can shock the person who falls in love with someone else, as well deeply upsetting their partner, as neither may have realised the degree to which their relationship had been in trouble before this. By the time an affair happens, there has usually been a great deal of accumulated unacknowledged hurt.

Whenever a couple is confronted by this situation, where one has had an affair or has fallen in love with someone else, it is vital to share with each other any resentments, angers, hurts and pain from the very beginning of the relationship, taking as long as is needed. Everything is included in this process – the deep wounds, such as not feeling desired sexually, to more everyday irritations, such as not cleaning the bath. Once the buried anger and hurt have been released, what is lying underneath becomes apparent. The key question is whether you still want to be together or not. If you do, then the next question is whether you love each other enough to go through what will inevitably be a painful journey, to find the ways in which you have disappointed, let down and hurt each other throughout the relationship. However, it is often hard to know whether you still love each other until after the accumulated resentment and hurt has been released.

We cannot let something go until we have experienced it fully. Otherwise this is another form of denial. There is no point, for example, in forgiving each other until we have first experienced how angry we are. The forgiveness is not real otherwise, and will not last very long without its roots in our true energy. If we try to reach our feelings of love without first engaging with our feelings of dislike, boredom, anger, sadness, fear, loss and so on, our experience of love will be insubstantial and weak. It is the very raw reality of our feelings, whatever they are, that in fact feed love. There is only one way to keep love alive and that is to be real. 'I love you' has a deeper resonance when you can say with equal freedom 'I hate you'.

One way to help release repressed feelings that have built up into a barrier between you is to link into the love-body of the relationship and to say: 'I resent (your partner's name, or "he" or "she") for . . .'.then say whatever you wish. If nothing comes to you, then simply repeat the first part of the sentence until something does. If nothing at all comes to you, then you may need the help of a counsellor or bodyworker to connect you with your buried feelings. You can do this in turn, simultaneously or one after the other. After doing this for 10 minutes, complete the sentences 'I'm afraid of...', and then 'I need...' in the same way. Again refer to your partner by name or in the third person. This is a helpful exercise, even if there is no crisis, as it dissolves what may be gradually accumulating between you before it becomes a problem. It's an emotional workout that keeps the relationship body healthy.

If we are emotionally closer to someone other than our partner, this is a sign that your love needs attention

Having an affair will usually put a relationship into crisis, but so will other situations where one is more intimate with another than they are with their partner. When we seek emotional closeness with someone other than our partner, such as a friend, a family member, a child or another lover, this can be the result of many factors. It may be a way of avoiding direct communication with our partner. It may be the result of many years of disappointment and failure to communicate with our partner and so we turn elsewhere for intimacy. Or maybe we never really loved our partner in the first place. It may also be that we are afraid of the deepening intimacy and commitment with our partner and have gone for an easier option. Any number of dynamics may be at work here. However, the *meaning* of the affair or deeper closeness with another can be seen as love trying to call attention to a serious imbalance somewhere in the relationship.

One way people can avoid real communication with each other is to become emotionally closer to one of their children than to their partner. This can look like parental love but it is, in fact, using the child's innocent instinctual bonding to avoid our adult responsibilities to make our own love. One of the symmetries I have seen many times is when one partner has an affair, often the man, and the other, often the woman, has been overly emotionally intimate with one or more of the children.

Love's most intimate messages come through the phenomena of daily life

If we do not listen to verbal communications they become emotional, and if we ignore these they will become behavioural. If we refuse to listen to these, then either our partners will leave or the message will become phenomenological.

Intimate phenomenological communications are the hardest to decipher. These might be an illness or a disease, an accident, a sexual problem, or a recurring situation that appears to be out of our control. These all have meanings, but usually ones that we least want to face. A communication that we want to hear will be understood long before it mutates into these less-conscious forms of expression.

Generally we ignore the meaning of most phenomena in our lives and think we are victims of events, but this is not the deeper truth. Life is not random. Illness, for example, has its origins in the energy of our body. More diseases are caused by our inability to protect ourselves than by the viruses themselves, as viruses and bacteria are everywhere, but we do not *all* succumb. Difficulties in fighting off predatory organisms are the consequence of behavioural habits as well as genetic predisposition. Habits, over time, create energetic imbalances within our bodies – metabolic, structural, hormonal, neurological, or whatever. Illness, therefore, has a phenomenological meaning that needs interpreting emotionally, behaviourally and spiritually as well as medically and scientifically.

Accidents, too, have their origin in part in some energetic disturbance somewhere within us. In some states in the US, after a traffic violation, you attend a re-education seminar. The day begins with the cop asking everyone to think back to the morning of their offence and to notice that some part of them, however small, *knew* they were going to have an accident or would violate some traffic regulation that day. Even though they knew this, they ignored the inner warning. How much more true is this likely to be of what happens within our intimate sexual relationships?

When our love speaks to us through phenomenological messages, these often have meanings we do not want to hear. If we had really wanted to we would have heard love's quieter whispers, long before they become concrete, in the form of something happening to our bodies or events in our lives. Let's look at a few examples.

Sexual dysfunction

Unless there is a physical problem, which in itself will have a meaning for the relationship, then there will be some dynamic giving rise to this. Maybe sex is being seen by one as a way to release tension and gratify a physical desire rather than an expression of love through the body, while the other is unconsciously feeling used and resentful of this. Maybe one partner is unconsciously withholding sex because the other is withholding some other aspect of themselves, and there is a hidden power battle involved. Perhaps our sexuality has been dominated by ideas of how it should be expressed, and has vanished to escape such mind control. Perhaps one is angry with the other, but has repressed it, feeling afraid of the intensity of their rage. But when we repress and deny our anger, we diminish our sexuality. Perhaps one is depressed and is not dealing with the causes of their feelings in relation to their partner. Perhaps . . . And so it goes on. It is useful sometimes to have a counsellor help uncover these hidden dynamics, but the primary factor is our willingness to find out the truth about what is going on, however painful.

An accident

Our unconscious energies are powerful forces that make things happen without our being aware of it. The energetic matrix underlying all the events of our lives is our own energy field. The energy field of our relationships is even more powerful. The source of an accident is in these energy fields. We describe things as due to chance only when we cannot see the underlying pattern or deeper grammar. Perhaps we felt trapped and powerless to change things. An accident will manifest this externally for us. Perhaps we needed to return to a level of helpless need and to be looked after for reasons we do not yet know. Perhaps we wanted to hurt our partner by hurting ourselves. Perhaps... Only you and your partner can find the hidden truth, as only you know the secrets of your own relationship.

No money

For one person, having no money means freedom, while for another, shame. For one it means an adventure, for another restriction. First find the meaning of money for yourself and your partner. Does money mean security, power, survival, success, pleasure, status, freedom, prison, fun or a burden? Then find out what having no money means for you both. Also try to discover what part of either of you wanted this to happen and why.

One way to find the meaning of an event, in this case having no money, is to make a list together of all the consequences – selling the house, cancelling a holiday, moving to a new area, changing work, and so on. Then sit side by side and examine together the possible benefits of each for your relationship.

When we surrender to the reality of our own experience and stop trying to control it, another level of love can come through

What I am saying is that the energy field of love between intimate sexual partners is so powerful that it can bring into material reality events and situations that are exactly what are needed to nurture the love. You may have to try this kind of exercise taking this on faith to begin with. It dawns slowly that this is what is happening, though for some people it can be a moment of satori-like revelation.

Before you experience love at work through phenomena in this way, it may all sound like New Age nonsense or psychobabble. All I can say is try it. If it does not work for you then it is not the case for you, though I suggest you give it time and don't just abandon the possibility quickly. After all, if it is the truth, then what a difference it will make.

In our materialist Western culture, which is most of the world now, we tend to conceive of happiness as something out there to be pursued. To this end we have developed powerful technologies that we hope will give us what will make us happy. This includes not only machines that deal with physical realities, but psychological technologies that tell us what to do and the steps to go through in order to get whatever power, wisdom, enlightenment, peace or love, etc, that we want.

This technological way of achieving certain inner experiences ignores a different way of being that sees happiness as part of our natural heritage that needs protecting, rather than out there to be found. And when we stop running around pursuing happiness, when we are still and silent, we find a different happiness. There are certain aspects to life that we can only know when we are vulnerable to them, not when we have power over them, such as our interdependence with each other, our fellowship with other animals, the power of the land and a respect for the mysteries of death. To know and experience these requires that we be vulnerable and surrender to our experience, not maintain a manipulative control of it. Love periodically reminds us that, however powerful we are in the world, in relation to love there needs to be vulnerability and surrender. The meaning of phenomena is often about the need to surrender to love rather than trying to develop more power over love, which is partly why our minds have difficulty understanding this.

Sexual love makes us more vulnerable than any other love

The deeper realities of love come to us through our experiences, our relationships and the phenomena of life around us – in other words, through our bodies. Talking and reading about love is most useful when it points us towards our actual experience. We all have to surrender eventually to the ultimate reality of experience anyway, whatever we may think about it. And the source of this is the body. All experience has its origins in the sensation and feeling of the body. The sexuality of love is therefore very potent. It creates subtle and powerful energies flowing through our bodies, and these more vulnerable, less-conscious aspects of being human become much more intense.

The most intimate vulnerability and surrender of all is to the reality of ourselves. And the truth we discover, if we experience ourselves deeply, is that we love. We love ourselves, we love others, and we love life – all life. And love is a state of being, not something we do.

As long as we are alive, we cannot escape love. Being willing to suffer the pains of existence is itself an act of love. Unconditional love, which embraces all experience and allows everything to be, is in all of us, just as it is in all life. But in most of us it remains unconscious and lives only in the dark interior of our bodies. Very few realise the truth of this love consciously, though lovers catch a glimpse every now and then, especially when making love.

The greatest love allows all things the freedom to be themselves

When we surrender to the truth of our love, it makes us vulnerable to *everything*. We begin to love our partners as they are, without demanding that they change. We love them unconditionally *and* we love ourselves in the same way. We let ourselves be and we let our partners be. We still get angry, afraid, upset, irritated and so on, but we no longer interfere with ourselves or our partners. We may control what we do but not who we are.

Unconditional love is not about having only positive feelings towards one another. That is impossible if you also want to make love. Sexual love involves the body, the unconscious – everything lives in the body. We can therefore avoid nothing in sexual relationships, and anyway why would we want to? Unconditional love allows everything the freedom to be, including what might be called 'unloving'. We may well want our partners to be different, feel angry with them and tell them so, but this becomes information about our love, about the relationship, rather than messages to them about what is wrong with them. There is a world of difference between saying 'I want to hurt you', which is information, and 'You are stupid', which is an attack. If you make enough love, there comes a time when you do not even have to control yourselves to this extent. You, your partner and the relationship are *absolutely* free. Your love is so vast it contains it all.

Several spiritual and psychological systems see everything in our life as an external manifestation of our inner reality, ourselves reflected back to us through what happens so that we can come to know ourselves; and that this is the deeper meaning of all phenomena. Some say everything we experience is us anyway, there is no separation. Others say our experience is an illusion, maya, as true reality is beyond the senses and the material. Some say that what happens is the unfolding of pre-ordained fate – destiny. Others maintain that we create the future each moment with our freewill. These are all ways of describing various aspects of experience and reality, and giving meaning to the phenomena of life. Sometimes it is helpful to think one way, sometimes another. They are different descriptions/interpretations of the same truth – life. Whatever name we give to what is greater than us, it is beyond anything we can comprehend. We can only be vulnerable to it, experience it, surrender to it and live it. As one tradition says, 'There is no God but God'. Or, as DH Lawrence said, 'There is no God apart from poppies and the flying fish'. Or as lovers might say, 'God is love'.

Practical exercises

Attuning to the subtle messages from your partner, your love and the phenomena of life, requires practice. Here are some exercises that will help you.

1   Have mornings where you sit in bed, before the day with its demands presses on you, and talk about your future together. What would you like if you could have everything you want?

2   Again, in the morning, before our more practical minds grab hold of us, share

what you would do if you had all the power in the world. What would you create, and what would you destroy? Imagine yourselves doing this together. You are likely to be surprised where this exercise takes you, especially if you stick at it for some time.

3   When you have failed to find a solution to a problem, use the power of your relationship to help you. First, sit together linking the body of your love and share your difficulties in detail. The other listens without offering practical solutions or sympathy, but instead shares any pictures or stray thoughts that come to them. You then see how these relate to your problem. For example, one might say, 'I'm worried about my job. I don't get on with my manager'. The other might say, 'I just got a picture of you lying on the beach'. You then find out what this might mean by lying on the floor and seeing how you feel. What pictures or thoughts do you get? And so on. This is an experiential investigation, not an intellectual one.

4   Both breathe deeply, relax and close your eyes. Count to three then open your eyes simultaneously. Tell each other the first thing your attention focuses on. For example, 'I saw the picture of the boat on the wall', or 'I noticed the stain on the carpet'. Then both explore together what this might mean. What does a boat mean to you? Freedom, danger, escape, relaxation . . . ? What does the stain mean? Housework, imperfection, a stain on your character, the party where wine was spilt, your home needing attention . . . ? Repeat this process several times, building up a picture of some of the unconscious dynamics in the relationship. This is especially useful if you are stuck when trying to work something out between you.

5   Sit in a cafe, on a train, up a mountain . . . and share with each other what you notice. See if the content and the differences have any relevance for your relationship.

6   Read each other's Tarot, throw the I Ching, have your astrological charts done, read the future in tea leaves . . . You don't have to know what you're doing, just make it up. The interpretation you give something is your own creation in response to the stimulus 'out there'. The meaning is to be found in the relationship between you and what you observe, not in the event, sign, card, coins or whatever themselves. And neither is it solely in yourself.

7   Sit side by side facing the body of your love, having agreed how long to do this exercise. Hold hands and close your eyes. When it feels right, release your hands and continue until the time is finished. Share any pictures, thoughts, feelings or memories that came to you. Do not try to work out what they mean at this point, but let yourself ponder on them through the day until an idea occurs to you about what they might mean.

8   Lie on your backs, close your eyes, breathe deeply and relax. Imagine you are

sailing out to sea, just the two of you. The shore gradually disappears. You are surrounded on all sides by sea. You take off your clothes and dive into the ocean. You can breathe underwater and continue swimming down. Down and down, until you reach the deep waters where there is hardly any light. What happens? If you want to, dive even deeper into the absolute darkness. Let the adventure unfold through your active imagination. Return to the boat and back to land. Share what happened. Were you together or alone? Did you meet any other creature? Did you find anything? Did you bring anything back?

9 Use different ways to communicate and experience yourselves and each other. Draw how you feel – your fear, your love, the relationship, the future, your body, your partner's body, and so on. Share the pictures and tell each other what you see. Enact dramas connected with your life together and the future you hope to create. Make music that expresses your love and your conflict. Use movement and voice as well as words and verbal language. Use any media that appeals to you to explore and express the energy of your love and your relationship.

10 If one of you needs help to make a decision, call on the energy field of your love to help you. Sit side by side facing your love. Honour your love in some way – bow down, be still and silent for while, say hello in some way, offer a symbolic gift, or do whatever suits you. Then ask for a sign. Notice what happens that day. Look for a sign and you will find one. Even not finding a sign is a message, perhaps suggesting you trust your own instincts and nothing else. You can do this alone, as your love and the love of the relationship will be present with or without your partner next to you.

11 Share your dreams every day. If you do not remember your dreams, then teach yourself to:

- Drink half a glass of water before you go to sleep. First thing in the morning, drink the other half. While drinking try to remember anything, however unformed.
- Have a notebook and pen beside the bed. On waking, before you do anything else, sit and write something. Even if it is only, 'There was nothing' or 'A vague feeling was around'.
- Before going to sleep sit in bed and meditate for five minutes. Longer than that is probably not possible!
- Last thing at night, hold hands with your partner and ask your love to help you remember your dreams.

12 If you don't start remembering at least a few dreams in a couple of weeks then it is likely there is a fear preventing you. This fear of the unknown parts of yourself will be manifesting itself in some form or other within your relationship. Perhaps you refuse to enter into real dialogue, you have an inability to be truly intimate, or you have an addiction or compulsion of some kind. To help you begin to deal with your fear and uncover your deeper self, ask your partner, use Linking exercises, visit a counsellor, or get some advice from someone you trust.

13 Notice any unusual sights and strange coincidences. Pay attention to any animals that cross your path. Listen to your own impulses and instincts. Give these any meaning you wish. This is a playful process and does not need to be deadly serious, even though surprising and revealing insights can arise.

14 Sit side by side, sitting in your love. Close your eyes and just feel. Feel the energy of the whole situation – yourselves, your partner, and everything around you. Stay together in this, past the point where you would normally stop. Be simply still and feel and listen to the energies.

CHAPTER EIGHTEEN

Love's Body

We laugh as love kills us
with honey and sugar and sweets.
Because love kills only the very best.
The secret is in killing you,
love bestows a hundred lives.
Enough!
I must not tell any more of love's secrets.
RUMI

The love that grows between two people who fall in love then try to build a life together is as profound as it is mysterious. This is why, as well as being wonderful, inspiring and nourishing, it is also tumultuous, challenging and chaotic. Anything in life that we commit ourselves to, engage in wholeheartedly and are deeply intimate with, will prove to be disturbing and difficult as well as fulfilling and satisfying, simply because this is how life is. Yet when our lives involve making money, bringing up children, building a career, nurturing friendships, and ensuring that we have good times as well as bad, then we need at least one place where we can simply be ourselves, without having to do what is appropriate, constructive, responsible, or whatever. A place where we get what we need *and* be spontaneously ourselves.

I am suggesting that the love created between lovers committed to building a life together can provide exactly this. Anything that comes between you – conflicts and fights, inner turmoil, anxieties and insecurities not eased by talking, misunderstandings and differences that divide you – can be resolved by simply bringing them in front of your love. By linking into and sharing everything with the body of your love, you are inviting your love to resolve things for you, which it will. You do not need to work on yourself or your partner, just get out of your own way and be vulnerable to love and it will all happen.

The more we allow our love to inform and nourish us, the stronger we become in ourselves. This means that we are more confident, do not doubt ourselves, and have an intrinsic trust in our own worth and natural 'goodness'. And so do our partners. Our disagreements and arguments then become even more intense, as the more we trust ourselves and our own experience, the less we are convinced by the arguments of others. This makes it even more important to link into to a wisdom greater than the two individuals, as the deeper truth is that neither one has the whole picture. Acknowledging your limitations, while maintaining the strength of your convictions, and linking into the greater wisdom of your love, allows many more things to happen between you. In other words, you are free to be completely yourself *and* to be deeply in intimate relationship with another.

You can resolve fights by asking what is love trying to teach you, rather than trying always to change or resist the other. You can tap into love's greater wisdom by simply laying out in front of your love all the many aspects of a situation until a new understanding or experience arrives, which it will. You can use your love as a mediator and interpreter, by talking to your love and not directly to each other. You can let your love absorb the full force of your feelings so that you do not overwhelm each other. In dire straits you can call out to your love for help, and love will always respond. Or you can simply sit together in the energy field of your love and let love do whatever it needs to.

This may sound simple, which it is, but the first step, being vulnerable and surrendering to love, is difficult for most of us. Our sophisticated technologies have given us a false sense of omnipotence, both in the outer world of material things and in the inner world of thoughts and feelings. We think we can achieve anything we want to once we know what to do. Sexual love shows us unequivocally that this is not the case, and that the areas of our lives that need us to surrender, be vulnerable and let go cannot be controlled and manipulated by our powerful skills, programs of action or affirmative self-belief.

Paradoxically, what I am also saying is that when we fall in love we have surrendered to love anyway. A Japanese soldier was found hiding in the jungle, still fighting World War Two, 40 years after the war had ended. The news that the war was over had not reached him. Similarly, the news that we have already surrendered to love has yet to reach us, that's all. What we are afraid of happening when we let go control and allow love to guide us – for example, that we will lose our individuality, freedom and self-determination, that our partners will leave us, not love us and take us for a ride, that our lives will become predictable, boring and routine, that we will go mad or become incapable – will prove to be phantoms. What is more, when we allow love to enter our lives, we discover a deeper happiness than can be obtained by any other means.

We may not know why we feel happy – it may remain simply as a feeling in our bodies and never spoken about at all – but we have an aura around us, a glow of inner happiness. We are simply living in the energy field of love.

We tend to imagine that the radiance surrounding lovers who have just fallen in love passes in time, that being in love is only for new lovers, yet this aura of love can become the climate of our lives, the atmosphere in which we live. There is an energy that surrounds couples who have been through many struggles and adventures together and yet remain deeply in love. It is very rare, but the energy field of love around such a couple can be felt by us all. And we instinctively know it to be something sacred.

Sexual love takes us right into the heart of the human mystery

To understand the truth of love, we do not have to consciously know about the complexities and depths of love and relationships. In fact, this is impossible. One person alone is complicated enough, two are more than double the complexity. It is enough to keep making love, then that love will do it all for us. I am just describing here some of the hidden treasures of sexual love as a form of poetry, if you like. Some of us give voice to these undercurrents, the mysteries lying beneath, the hidden spring that gives nourishment and meaning to it all, most do not. And by far the most important thing is to embody love, not to write or talk about it, especially as words find their meaning through the body anyway.

If what I say has meaning for you, it is simply because you already know it. Perhaps you haven't yet realised that you do, that's all. And sexual love has many more mysteries to reveal than we can ever realise consciously anyway.

By making love we are participating in the greatest mystery of all, that of love in the body and the endless re-creation of love in life. When we surrender to the pleasures of sexual love, our bodies, in their deeper instinctive wisdom, know the full truth about love, even when our minds have no idea. We move through our inhibitions and fears and become more alive, more present, more loving. We laugh, enjoy life more and love more deeply. We discover the wisdom of the body. We find we are beautiful animals with a glorious instinctual heritage. We encounter profound truths of life on this planet. The revelations of sexual love take us right into the heart of our human mystery.

The first revelation of sexual love is the wisdom of the body

We think of the body as an object, but the body is not a thing – it is a continuous creation, a constant flow of energy. For a baby, everything is one body, out of which comes the great division into many. We have created the idea of an object out of the flow of energy that is the real life of the body. And the body, as we think of it, is a cultural creation, a body politic, where the head rules as a monarch. We then think wisdom lies in the brain, and allow our heads to rule our hearts. But there is a far deeper, older wisdom in our bodies.

Our bodies hold a map of the history of life on Earth, not only, as we have seen, our personal history. The greatest story ever told, the story of life on Earth, is reflected in our bones. In our growth in the womb, from a single cell dividing into two, we embody the process of evolution. Shadows of gills, wings and webbed feet appear then disappear, and rudimentary tails and horns emerge and fade until we leave our saltwater home and struggle to take our first breath on land. This leaves us with a cellular memory of all our ancestors that preceded us – people who were born, lived, struggled and died so that we might live. And greater love than this does not exist. Deep within our bodies lives a profound respect for these unknown ancestors, our biological parents.

Sexual love connects us with our essential Earth nature and our true family because it connects us with our instincts, the universal language of all life. The more we make love, the more our instinctive and natural love for life emerges from deep within our cells. It has been waiting here to be released ever since we left the Eden of our innocent instinctual love of all life, before we divided life in order to rule over it. Sexual love takes us back into paradise, the Garden of Eden that our beautiful animal bodies never left, and in doing so reveals what life on Earth is really worth.

The second revelation of sexual love is the holy communion of all life

Through sexual love we experience the truth that our bodies are alive, that we are animals and, whatever we may think, that our body is a flow of energy, a body electric. Melting into the pleasures of sex, dissolving into the sensations and feeling of the body, we become one with our partner, a continuous flow of energy that cannot be divided. We slowly realise that this is a truth with meaning for all bodies.

We may think we are superior, occupying a unique position at the top of creation, owing nothing to any other species but our own, but in the dark interior of the body we know better. We recognise the other animals as our brothers and sisters, our mothers and fathers, our cousins and our fellows. Our bodies know that we belong to the great family of all life on Earth. Under the skin, Earth species are not so very different. Though the arrangements of our organs might differ, warm-blooded creatures all have hearts, and if you prick any mammal does it not bleed? Every breath is a reminder that we are like all the other animals that breathe, whether through lungs, gills or osmosis. That we eat them and they eat us is the holy communion of life.

Everything alive is in a constant flow with everything else. In sexual love this is not an abstract idea but a direct experience. Sexual love reveals to us the full glorious paradox, that we are each of us, every living creature, unique, different, individual, separate and distinct, while at the same time being interdependent, interconnected and flowing into each other in a dance of energies, where we are all one.

The energetic source of this great river, and the ocean into which it flows, has been given many names – the Tao, the Dhamma, God, Allah, Nirvana, the quantum energy field, Dreamtime . . . Lovers know it by another name – love. The second revelation of sexual love is that all life is ultimately one, and this holy communion is the ultimate reality of love from which we came and into which we will return.

The third revelation of sexual love is that our love will live forever

By going into the darkness of our bodies through sexual love and discovering the hidden truths that lie waiting for us there, we expand our sense of who and what we are to include energies and realities far beyond our personalities. We find an infinity of possibilities lies within us. We feel ourselves as energies, rather than thinking of ourselves as individuals. Our ego, our personality, becomes just a part of our identity, not our whole being. All this takes us to another level of understanding of what it means to be human.

We realise that who and what we are is not confined to our thoughts, memories, hopes, fears, beliefs, and personal likes and dislikes. These are all aspects of our life that will die when we die, that will live on in the hearts of those who knew us, but will no longer have their own independent existence. Other energies of life we have embodied will continue, however, long after we have died. The energies that live outside time and space, that are not of this world, that are connected with the worlds of energy and the spirit, that transcend our temporal existence, aspects of what has been called our soul, all these are eternal.

Only the separate ego dies – the personality, the individual identity. Our love survives our death as it is a force greater than our individual ego and is connected with the source of life itself. Whatever we have loved enough to be willing to die for will be in life forever. As we say goodbye to life at our death, all the love there has ever been in our heart pours back into life. If we have loved freedom, that will be what we give back to life when we die. If we have loved beauty, then that, too, will resonate in existence forever. If we have loved nothing enough to die for it, then that will be what we leave behind us – nothing. And if we have loved life, then though our body may die, our love lives on in life forever.

The fourth revelation of sexual love is the spirituality of the body

The sacred is not apart from life – it is life. Sexual love shows us that what has been called sacred, mystical and spiritual is the rightful inheritance of everybody alive, not confined to religions, priests, shamans and dead people. Whenever we make love, we bring love into the body, into physical reality and into matter, and love is incarnated and made flesh by us and through us. Sexual love brings the redemptive energy of love into life, into the body. And when love is alive in the very cells of our bodies, we have a presence, a vitality and an integrity that is nothing to do with what is generally accepted as goodness or holiness.

This wholeness, this integrity, this love in the body, is what is really holy. A disembodied set of ideas can never be as real or as good as love in the body. The spirit of love must arrive in the body, not the body ascend to the spirit. As the Tantric Buddhas have told us: 'This very Body the Buddha, this very Earth the Lotus Paradise'. And when we are making love, moaning with pleasure, sighing with delight, moving with ecstatic abandon, laughing with the joy of it, then we know this, too. We know that making love is the most sacred and profound human act. We know that our bodies, made from the love-making of our parents, are incarnated love, love made flesh. We know that all life is sacred. And we know that our bodies are of love, that love's body is everybody.

Love's Body is us

For most of us, these deeper realities are experienced not in thoughts that can be put into words, but as pleasures and experiences in the body. It is the work of mystics, musicians, poets, dancers, shamans, creative writers, singers and other artists to put these experiences into form, into words. For the rest of us, we simply need to let the pleasures and experiences of sexual love do their work in teaching our bodies how to love. This love will then show itself through our actions, through the way we behave with our partners, through what we create, through our care for children and animals, through our presence and energy, through our integrity and through our love.

It is more important for us to learn how to love each other than it is for us to become amazing, have everything we want, live in a constant state of bliss, be free from fear, enlightened, or whatever other goal we set ourselves. Any ideal we impose on ourselves and our partners will interfere with who and what we are, and it is through the reality of ourselves that we live and love, not through our perfection. Sexual love teaches us how to love each other in our less-than-perfect humanity. And there is no other way to love.

As we make more love, its energy field expands and gradually spreads throughout our life. We act with an integrity that affirms and supports life, not condemning or rejecting the spontaneous realities of life all around us. We naturally reach out to help others, our children and animals. We expand our sense of self to include others. We continue to make love. Love slowly fills the very cells of our bodies, where it redeems and transforms not only our own history but the history of life on Earth. Through the sexuality of love, we discover that the energy of the body can never die; it is always transformed into more life. Fear dies, the separate ego dies, the personality dies, but life itself does not die. We come to eternal life through the animal body, through the sexuality of love, through the endless transformation of life into life. We become the body of our love.

Sexual love is the sacramental experience, the sacred coming together that reveals the unconscious truth, hidden in the vast darkness of the body, which is that there is only one body – the body of all of us. As the hero in a great Apache legend announces: 'This earth is my body. The sky is my body. The seasons are my body. The water is my body. It is the truth that these are all my body'. Sexual love reveals the holy communion of life, that we are all one body, members of each other. The great truth at the heart of sexual love is that this body is love. Love's Body is everybody. We are Love's Body. Love's Body is this – all of it.

CHAPTER NINETEEN

12 Steps Using Your Love to Create the Relationship You Long For

You can do this exercise when you haven't got a partner, and your beloved is someone unknown to you, or when you are with a partner and are longing for more with them. But be aware that the relationship you long for is not necessarily the same as the one you think you want. So be prepared to be surprised.

1. Imagine the body of your love is in front of you, on a cushion or an empty chair. Link into your love as if it were a real presence in front of you (which, of course, it is). If it helps, close your eyes.

2. Imagine the one you love sitting next to you, also facing the love-body, even though you may not know who they are.

3. Speak aloud to your love-body about how you feel in the situation with the three of you sitting together. It is important to speak aloud as this brings your body into what you say. 'I feel comfortable, curious, afraid, familiar, embarrassed', or whatever.

4. Speak to the love-body about the physical absence of the one you love, both the positive and negative aspects. For example, 'I feel relieved they cannot hear me speak. And I also feel sad'. There is always a degree of ambivalence even if you do not initially realise this, so give yourself time to find the less-familiar feelings.

5. Speak about your hopes and fears. Both.

6. Say what you want from whoever is beside you, again speaking to the love-body in front of you. Say what you really want, not only what you think you should want. For example, 'I want him to be wealthy and successful' or 'I want her to be slim and beautiful'.

7. Say what you want from the relationship. 'I want to be supported.' 'I want deeply enjoyable sex.'

8. Say what you want, this time in the form of what you want to experience. 'I want to feel secure.' 'I want to feel alive.' This step is the most important.

9. Give your needs and wants over to your love to sort out for you. If it helps, imagine them in a bag that you give to the love-body. Then let them go. Your active part

has finished. Now let love do the work of bringing your longing for love into form.

10 Sit and feel the three of you together, and see if there is anything else you want to say about yourself, your absent lover, your love, or anything else.

11 Sit with your eyes closed, feeling the two of you surrounded by the energy field of your love. Be in love.

12 In whatever way feels right to you, honour your love.

Do this routine daily for 10-15 minutes, and your beloved will eventually appear. You may find it is another person, yourself, God, an animal, nature, or something else entirely. Our love evolves as we do, so keep doing this exercise daily and you will find it changes. The very act, for example, of connecting with our love immediately changes things, and who or what we love may also change. Eventually, your love will draw into form a manifestation of your love. Our authority lies in stating what we want. Our surrender lies in accepting the form in which love brings it to us. Good luck!

Some Patterns of Synchronicity, Symmetry, Balance, Equivalence and Dynamic Homeostasis found in Loving Relationships

1 An apparent strength in one partner reveals its hidden weakness at the same time an apparent weakness in the other reveals its strength.

2 Any power dynamic operating one way has an equal dynamic operating the other way, though this is often hidden.

3 The balance of power in a relationship remains equal as long as the couple remains together.

4 The power in one will be experienced by the other in both its creative and its destructive forms.

5 What attracts a couple initially is what will later threaten to split them apart.

6 Unresolved conflicts between the parents of each will re-emerge between the couple.

7 We fall in love with what has the potential to break our hearts open. In other words, what we most long for is also what will cause us the deepest suffering.

8 There are alternating cycles of power and vulnerability throughout the relationship, first one having the power, the other the vulnerability, then the other way around. The balance of power equalises over time.

9 The level of difference and conflict that emerges in a relationship is directly related to the amount of love.

10 The amount of love generated in a relationship is directly related to the degree of difference allowed.

11 The more love is made in a relationship, the more aspects of each will be revealed. And the more that is revealed, the more love is made.

12 As a new energy arrives in the relationship through one, there is a synchronous emergence of a corresponding energy in the other.

13 If two people are in love then although they may not always get what they want, they will always get what they need.

14 Each has what the other needs for healing, but also what will hurt them.

15 The degree of engagement in making love – the amount of energy, presence, inquiry, commitment, and how much each gives to the relationship – is equal over time for both partners. In other words, the capacity for love is equal.

16 Every resolution of conflict creates a deeper love which in turn allows a deeper level of conflict to emerge, and so on.

17 The wounds that each bring to the relationship have the same degree of suffering in them, though usually very different in form.

18 Love transforms itself into its highest fulfillment by expanding until it can include its polar opposite. What was outside the love becomes contained within it. The attraction of opposites ensures love grows.

19 The way to find your true partner for these patterns is to follow your sexual energy. The body and the instincts are then making the choice, and the unconscious wisdom of the body is attuned to these things.

20 The opposing polarities between you progressively expand to include more and more of reality.

21 Every hell you redeem between you takes you into another paradise, from which you are ejected all over again.

22 Each inducts the other into worlds in which they are the master and the other is an apprentice.

23 These worlds are equally important and significant.

24 Any fixed, non-negotiable rule will be repeatedly challenged by your love.

25 The one that apparently initiates a change in the dynamics/agreements of the relationship or lifestyle may not be the one that has really instigated it.

26 The one who really instigates it is the one that has been most frustrated or hurt in the previous dynamic/agreements.

27 Any contract or agreement is a temporary support until the love of the relationship is strong enough to handle another level of reality.

28 Love is always attempting to heal something even if there is a war between the partners. But love can't always complete its purpose in one lifetime or one relationship.

29 Partners always know each other's vulnerabilities, which gives them power over each other.

30 The differences are where there's conflict and also where you make the love.

31 Love creates the context for the widest healing of family, society, earth, etc.

32 The primary dynamic in any family is the nature of the relationship between the parents.

33 Each tends to give to the other what they themselves need and want rather than what their partner actually needs and wants. Eventually, the needs and wants of each gradually converge, and each needs the other as well as themselves to get what they need.

34 Each will give to the other any unresolved pain within them until there is enough love made to redeem it within themselves.

35 Being held by love will heal all hurt.

36 If an event leads to the couple separating then this is because their love was not strong enough to contain all the consequences. It is never the event per se.

37 The hopes and fears of each are continually evolving and changing yet continually jigsaw into each other. The hopes of one contain the fears of the other, and vice versa.

38 The stronger both become through their love, the more they are dependent upon their love to help them.

39 And their conflicts become more intense, though less personal.

40 The partner we are in love with is the partner that we long for though we may not know this.

Postscript

After writing this book, I found myself once more in a deep and painful fight with my partner. Neither of us could give way or compromise, as it felt that to do so would violate our integrity. The apparent issue we were struggling with was deceptively simple: whether to move home or not. But as with so many of our battles, there were layers and layers that revealed themselves.

There is an inescapable darkness in the human heart that is present in some form or other in every committed intimate sexual partnership and goes to the heart of our human condition. What I have called 'The Dark Marriage' cannot be avoided however much love we make. In fact, the more love we make, the deeper the darkness that can emerge. But the darkness that emerges within the context of love is contained and does not go on to cause more innocent suffering.

Most people are not aware of their inner darkness, yet the more unconscious we are of it, the more it becomes a force for harm. 'The Dark Marriage' emerges anyway in the vicious fights of the divorce courts, in the lack of real communication in many homes, in our betrayal of the body, in pressure on our children to save us from our own unhappiness rather than nurturing them to become themselves.

But if war is not the answer, neither is a war on war. Peace at any price may cost us more than a war, repressing further the realities that need to be engaged not buried. Our only hope is to create a love that can contain and allow the full reality of our human condition, including all its darkness. But to become conscious of the buried darkness in our hearts is very painful. There need to be special places where this can happen in ways that honour and protect the raw energies that will emerge and the profound vulnerability that paradoxically comes with them. The dynamic meditations of Osho, encounter groups, the Open Forums of Arnold and Amy Mindell, the Truth and Reconciliation Commission of South Africa, silent meditations where you feel everything and do nothing, Bioenergetics, Left-Handed Tantra, the Voice Dialogue of Hal and Sidra Stone, Veeresh's work at Humaniversity, all these and many others are routes through which we can encounter the truths of our human condition with its tremendous capacity for both good and evil. And one of the most potent of all is honesty and love in committed intimate sexual relationships.

The feeling witness that evolves through these various processes allows everything to be – life and death, good and evil, joy and suffering. The possibility of the human spirit to evolve a wisdom and love that embraces everything may be humanity's greatest creation – it may be that through this we collectively create the God we need to save us from ourselves. What is certain is that if we do not allow the energies and forces of our human darkness to have some form of expression, they will gather in the collective unconscious and emerge eventually in war. Currently we are facing another war. A different kind of war, but whether between nation states over territory, different vested interests over oil, or an unholy war between religions, there are now weapons of mass destruction on all sides that threaten us all. More than ever we need to find ways to consciously engage the dynamics between the various polarised and opposing positions, and release the trapped energies that divide us.

Over the next few weeks my partner and I began the painful process of uncovering yet more of the pains and struggles of our life together. We had, of course, done this many times before, but not with the same degree of bitterness, betrayal and despair that emerged this time. We continued into the more existential aspects of our core conflicts, between my fluidity and his solidity, my reaching out to create dialogue and his rooted standing his ground, my willingness to die into the situation and his fight for life. We brought everything to our love. As we continued we began to feel the forces at work around the globe emerging within and between us – the forces of religious fundamentalism, America, Europe, shifting alliances, the struggles in the Middle East. It was as if we were wrestling to find something other than war to reconcile the polarisations between us and this had implications for the world situation too. And it was very painful.

At one point we both felt we were not going to get through this and would separate. I was thinking I could no longer work with relationships – to do so would be phoney after my own spectacular failure. The book would have to go unpublished, my work over. My partner was going through his equivalent – that no matter how much he loved me, he was profoundly lonely and alone. Finally my heart broke open (again!) and I wept. I let go of everything – my relationship, my work, my home, my future dreams – and simply wept in front of love. Not even my love or our love by this time – simply love. My partner reached out to me and we re-met in love, though neither of us knew what the future would hold. Slowly our new life began to reveal itself. We found a new home. My work continues, but in a different way. The book would be published – you would not, of course, be reading it otherwise! And our life and love continues.

Hopefully our love contributes not only to our own happiness, but to others' too – just as their love contributes to ours; and through daring to love and be loved, all of us can make our contribution to the whole. And, dare I say it, make love not war.

Bibliography

Relationships

Stone, Hal and Sidra, *Partnering*, New World Library, 2000

Stone, Hal and Sidra, *Embracing Each Other*, Delos Inc, 1989

Stone, Hal and Sidra, *Embracing Your Inner Critic*, Harper San Francisco, 1993

Stone, Sidra, *The Shadow King*, Universal Publishers, 2000

Hellinger, Bert, *Love's Hidden Symmetry*, Zeig, Tucker and Co, 1998

Rowe, Dorothy, *Beyond Fear*, HarperCollins, 2002

Satir, Virginia, *The New People Making*, Science and Behaviour Books, 1988

Mindell, Arnold and Amy, *The Dreambody in Relationships*, Penguin Arkana, 1987

Mindell, Arnold and Amy, *Riding the Horse Backwards*, Penguin Arkana, 1992

Cappachione, Louise, *Recovery of Your Inner Child*, Simon & Schuster, 1991

The Body

Lowen, Alexander, *Bionenergetics*, Penguin Books, 1975

Lowen, Alexander, *Love, Sex, and Your Heart*, Macmillan, 1988

Reich, Withelm, *The Function of the Orgasm*, NY Orgone Inst Press, 1934

Roth, Gabrielle, *Sweat Your Prayers*, Newleaf, 1999

Energy

Osho, *The Tantra Experience*, Element, 1994

Sheldrake, Rupert, *Seven Experiments That Could Change the World*, Fourth Estate, 1994

McTaggart, Lynne, *The Field*, HarperCollins, 2001

Moss, Richard, *The Black Butterfly*, Celestial Arts, 1986

Moreno, JL, *The Essential Moreno*, Ed. J Fox, Springer, 1987

Quotes from Rumi's poetry taken from:

The Essential Rumi, Trans by C Barks with J Moyne, Harper San Francisco, 1995

Unseen Rain, J Moyne and C Barks, Threshold Books, 1986

Index